Waiting for godot

Other Works by Samuel Beckett
Published by Grove Press

Cascando and Other Short Dramatic Pieces
(Words and Music, Eh Joe, Play, Come and Go, Film
[original version])
Collected Poems in English and French
The Collected Works of Samuel Beckett [twenty-four volumes]
Company
Endgame
Ends and Odds
Film, A Film Script
First Love and Other Shorts
(From an Abandoned Work, Enough, Imagination and Dead
Imagine, Ping, Not I, Breath)
Fizzles
Happy Days
How It Is
I Can't Go On, I'll Go On: A Selection from Samuel Beckett's Work
Krapp's Last Tape and Other Dramatic Pieces
(All That Fall, Embers [a play for radio], Acts Without Words
I and II [mimes])
Ill Seen Ill Said
The Lost Ones
Malone Dies
Mercier and Camier
Molloy
More Pricks Than Kicks
Murphy
Poems in English
Proust
Rockaby and Other Short Pieces
Stories and Texts for Nothing
Three Novels
(Molloy, Malone Dies, The Unnamable)
The Unnamable
Watt

Waiting for godot

WAITING

FOR GODOT

tragicomedy in 2 acts

by samuel beckett

grove press, inc.

new york

First Evergreen Edition 1956
Sixty-third Printing 1982
ISBN: 0-394-17204-3
Library of Congress Catalog Card Number: 54-6803

Manufactured in the United States of America

GROVE PRESS, INC., 196 West Houston Street, New York, N.Y. 10014

Estragon

Vladimir

Lucky

Pozzo

a boy

ACT I

A country road. A tree.

Evening.

Estragon, sitting on a low mound, is trying to take off his boot. He pulls at it with both hands, panting. He gives up, exhausted, rests, tries again. As before.
Enter Vladimir.

ESTRAGON: (*giving up again*). Nothing to be done.

VLADIMIR: (*advancing with short, stiff strides, legs wide apart*). I'm beginning to come round to that opinion. All my life I've tried to put it from me, saying, Vladimir, be reasonable, you haven't yet tried everything. And I resumed the struggle. (*He broods, musing on the struggle. Turning to Estragon.*) So there you are again.

ESTRAGON: Am I?

VLADIMIR: I'm glad to see you back. I thought you were gone for ever.

ESTRAGON: Me too.

VLADIMIR: Together again at last! We'll have to celebrate this. But how? (*He reflects.*) Get up till I embrace you.

ESTRAGON: (*irritably*). Not now, not now.

VLADIMIR: (*hurt, coldly*). May one inquire where His Highness spent the night?

ESTRAGON: In a ditch

VLADIMIR: (*admiringly*). A ditch! Where?

ESTRAGON: (*without gesture*). Over there.

VLADIMIR: And they didn't beat you?

ESTRAGON: Beat me? Certainly they beat me.

VLADIMIR: The same lot as usual?

ESTRAGON: The same? I don't know.

VLADIMIR: When I think of it . . . all these years . . . **but** for me . . . where would you be . . . (*Decisively.*) You'd be nothing more than a little heap of bones at the present minute, no doubt about it.

ESTRAGON: And what of it?

VLADIMIR: (*gloomily*). It's too much for one man. (*Pause. Cheerfully.*) On the other hand what's the good of losing heart now, that's what I say. We should have thought of it a million years ago, in the nineties.

ESTRAGON: Ah stop blathering and help me off with this bloody thing.

VLADIMIR: Hand in hand from the top of the Eiffel Tower, among the first. We were respectable in those days. Now it's too late. They wouldn't even let us up. (*Estragon tears at his boot.*) What are you doing?

ESTRAGON: Taking off my boot. Did that never happen to you?

VLADIMIR: Boots must be taken off every day, I'm tired telling you that. Why don't you listen to me?

ESTRAGON: (*feebly*). Help me!

VLADIMIR: It hurts?

ESTRAGON: (*angrily*). Hurts! He wants to know if it hurts!

VLADIMIR: (*angrily*). No one ever suffers but you. I don't count. I'd like to hear what you'd say if you had what I have.

ESTRAGON: It hurts?

VLADIMIR: (*angrily*). Hurts! He wants to know if it hurts!

ESTRAGON: (*pointing*). You might button it all the same.

VLADIMIR: (*stooping*). True. (*He buttons his fly.*) Never neglect the little things of life.

ESTRAGON: What do you expect, you always wait till the last moment.

VLADIMIR: (*musingly*). The last moment . . . (*He meditates.*) Hope deferred maketh the something sick, who said that?

ESTRAGON: Why don't you help me?

VLADIMIR: Sometimes I feel it coming all the same. Then I go all queer. (*He takes off his hat, peers inside it, feels about inside it, shakes it, puts it on again.*) How shall I say? Relieved and at the same time . . . (*he searches for the word*) . . . appalled. (*With emphasis.*) AP-PALLED. (*He takes off his hat again, peers inside it.*) Funny. (*He knocks on the crown as though to dislodge a foreign body, peers into it again, puts it on again.*) Nothing to be done. (*Estragon with a supreme effort succeeds in pulling off his boot. He peers inside it, feels about inside it, turns it upside down, shakes it, looks on the ground to see if anything has fallen out, finds nothing, feels inside it again, staring sightlessly before him.*) Well?

ESTRAGON: Nothing.

VLADIMIR: Show.

ESTRAGON: There's nothing to show.

VLADIMIR: Try and put it on again.

ESTRAGON: (*examining his foot*). I'll air it for a bit.

VLADIMIR: There's man all over for you, blaming on his boots the faults of his feet. (*He takes off his hat again, peers inside it, feels about inside it, knocks on the crown, blows into it, puts it on again.*) This is getting alarming. (*Silence. Vladimir deep in thought, Estragon pulling at his toes.*) One of the thieves was saved. (*Pause.*) It's a reasonable percentage. (*Pause.*) Gogo.

ESTRAGON: What?

VLADIMIR: Suppose we repented.

ESTRAGON: Repented what?

VLADIMIR: Oh . . . (*He reflects.*) We wouldn't have to go into the details.

ESTRAGON: Our being born?
Vladimir breaks into a hearty laugh which he immediately stifles, his hand pressed to his pubis, his face contorted.

VLADIMIR: One daren't even laugh any more.

ESTRAGON: Dreadful privation.

VLADIMIR: Merely smile. (*He smiles suddenly from ear to ear, keeps smiling, ceases as suddenly.*) It's not the same thing. Nothing to be done. (*Pause.*) Gogo.

ESTRAGON: (*irritably*). What is it?

VLADIMIR: Did you ever read the Bible?

ESTRAGON: The Bible . . . (*He reflects.*) I must have taken a look at it.

VLADIMIR: Do you remember the Gospels?

ESTRAGON: I remember the maps of the Holy Land. Coloured they were. Very pretty. The Dead Sea was pale blue. The very look of it made me thirsty. That's where we'll go, I used to say, that's where we'll go for our honeymoon. We'll swim. We'll be happy.

VLADIMIR: You should have been a poet.

ESTRAGON: I was. (*Gesture towards his rags.*) Isn't that obvious?

Silence.

VLADIMIR: Where was I . . . How's your foot?

ESTRAGON: Swelling visibly.

VLADIMIR: Ah yes, the two thieves. Do you remember the story?

ESTRAGON: No.

VLADIMIR: Shall I tell it to you?

ESTRAGON: No.

VLADIMIR: It'll pass the time. (*Pause.*) Two thieves, crucified at the same time as our Saviour. One—

ESTRAGON: Our what?

VLADIMIR: Our Saviour. Two thieves. One is supposed to have been saved and the other . . . (*he searches for the contrary of saved*) . . . damned.

ESTRAGON: Saved from what?

VLADIMIR: Hell.

ESTRAGON: I'm going.

He does not move.

VLADIMIR: And yet . . . (*pause*) . . . how is it—this is not boring you I hope—how is it that of the four Evangelists only one speaks of a thief being saved. The four of them were there—or thereabouts—and only one speaks of a thief being saved. (*Pause.*) Come on, Gogo, return the ball, can't you, once in a way?

ESTRAGON: (*with exaggerated enthusiasm*). I find this really most extraordinarily interesting.

9

VLADIMIR: One out of four. Of the other three two don't mention any thieves at all and the third says that both of them abused him.

ESTRAGON: Who?

VLADIMIR: What?

ESTRAGON: What's all this about? Abused who?

VLADIMIR: The Saviour.

ESTRAGON: Why?

VLADIMIR: Because he wouldn't save them.

ESTRAGON: From hell?

VLADIMIR: Imbecile! From death.

ESTRAGON: I thought you said hell.

VLADIMIR: From death, from death.

ESTRAGON: Well what of it?

VLADIMIR: Then the two of them must have been damned.

ESTRAGON: And why not?

VLADIMIR: But one of the four says that one of the two was saved.

ESTRAGON: Well? They don't agree and that's all there is to it.

VLADIMIR: But all four were there. And only one speaks of a thief being saved. Why believe him rather than the others?

ESTRAGON: Who believes him?

VLADIMIR: Everybody. It's the only version they know.

ESTRAGON: People are bloody ignorant apes.

He rises painfully, goes limping to extreme left, halts, gazes into distance off with his hand screening his eyes, turns, goes to extreme right, gazes into distance. Vladimir watches him, then goes and picks up the boot, peers into it, drops it hastily.

VLADIMIR: Pah!

He spits. Estragon moves to center, halts with his back to auditorium.

ESTRAGON: Charming spot. (*He turns, advances to front, halts facing auditorium.*) Inspiring prospects. (*He turns to Vladimir.*) Let's go.

VLADIMIR: We can't.

ESTRAGON: Why not?

VLADIMIR: We're waiting for Godot.

ESTRAGON: (*despairingly*). Ah! (*Pause.*) You're sure it was here?

VLADIMIR: What?

ESTRAGON: That we were to wait.

VLADIMIR: He said by the tree. (*They look at the tree.*) Do you see any others.

ESTRAGON: What is it?

VLADIMIR: I don't know. A willow.

ESTRAGON: Where are the leaves?

VLADIMIR: It must be dead.

ESTRAGON: No more weeping.

VLADIMIR: Or perhaps it's not the season.

ESTRAGON: Looks to me more like a bush.

VLADIMIR: A shrub.

ESTRAGON: A bush.

VLADIMIR: A—. What are you insinuating? That we've come to the wrong place?

ESTRAGON: He should be here.

VLADIMIR: He didn't say for sure he'd come.

ESTRAGON: And if he doesn't come?

VLADIMIR: We'll come back to-morrow.

ESTRAGON: And then the day after to-morrow.

VLADIMIR: Possibly.

ESTRAGON: And so on.

VLADIMIR: The point is—

ESTRAGON: Until he comes.

VLADIMIR: You're merciless.

ESTRAGON: We came here yesterday.

VLADIMIR: Ah no, there you're mistaken.

ESTRAGON: What did we do yesterday?

VLADIMIR: What did we do yesterday?

ESTRAGON: Yes.

VLADIMIR: Why . . . (*Angrily.*) Nothing is certain when you're about.

ESTRAGON: In my opinion we were here.

VLADIMIR: (*looking round*). You recognize the place?

ESTRAGON: I didn't say that.

VLADIMIR: Well?

ESTRAGON: That makes no difference.

VLADIMIR: All the same . . . that tree . . . (*turning towards auditorium*) that bog . . .

ESTRAGON: You're sure it was this evening?

VLADIMIR: What?

ESTRAGON: That we were to wait.

VLADIMIR: He said Saturday. (*Pause.*) I think.

ESTRAGON: You think.

VLADIMIR: I must have made a note of it. (*He fumbles in his pockets, bursting with miscellaneous rubbish.*)

ESTRAGON: (*very insidious*). But what Saturday? And is it Saturday? Is it not rather Sunday? (*Pause.*) Or Monday? (*Pause.*) Or Friday?

VLADIMIR: (*looking wildly about him, as though the date was inscribed in the landscape*). It's not possible!

ESTRAGON: Or Thursday?

VLADIMIR: What'll we do?

ESTRAGON: If he came yesterday and we weren't here you may be sure he won't come again to-day.

VLADIMIR: But you say we were here yesterday.

ESTRAGON: I may be mistaken. (*Pause.*) Let's stop talking for a minute, do you mind?

VLADIMIR: (*feebly*). All right. (*Estragon sits down on the mound. Vladimir paces agitatedly to and fro, halting from time to time to gaze into distance off. Estragon falls asleep. Vladimir halts finally before Estragon.*) Gogo! . . . Gogo! . . . GOGO! *Estragon wakes with a start.*

ESTRAGON: (*restored to the horror of his situation*). I was asleep! (*Despairingly.*) Why will you never let me sleep?

VLADIMIR: I felt lonely.

ESTRAGON: I had a dream.

VLADIMIR: Don't tell me!

ESTRAGON: I dreamt that—

VLADIMIR: DON'T TELL ME!

ESTRAGON: (*gesture towards the universe*). This one is enough for you? (*Silence.*) It's not nice of you, Didi. Who am I to tell my private nightmares to if I can't tell them to you?

VLADIMIR: Let them remain private. You know I can't bear that.

ESTRAGON: (*coldly*). There are times when I wonder if it wouldn't be better for us to part.

VLADIMIR: You wouldn't go far.

ESTRAGON: That would be too bad, really too bad. (*Pause.*) Wouldn't it, Didi, be really too bad? (*Pause.*) When you think of the beauty of the way. (*Pause.*) And the goodness of the wayfarers. (*Pause. Wheedling.*) Wouldn't it, Didi?

VLADIMIR: Calm yourself.

ESTRAGON: (*voluptuously*). Calm . . . calm . . . The English say cawm. (*Pause.*) You know the story of the Englishman in the brothel?

VLADIMIR: Yes.

ESTRAGON: Tell it to me.

VLADIMIR: Ah stop it!

ESTRAGON: An Englishman having drunk a little more than usual proceeds to a brothel. The bawd asks him if he wants a fair one, a dark one or a red-haired one. Go on.

VLADIMIR: STOP IT!

Exit Vladimir hurriedly. Estragon gets up and follows him as far as the limit of the stage. Gestures of Estragon like those of a spectator encouraging a pugilist. Enter Vladimir. He brushes past Estragon, crosses the stage with bowed head. Estragon takes a step towards him, halts.

ESTRAGON: (*gently*). You wanted to speak to me? (*Silence. Estragon takes a step forward.*) You had something to say to me? (*Silence. Another step forward.*) Didi . . .

VLADIMIR: (*without turning*). I've nothing to say to you.

ESTRAGON: (*step forward*). You're angry? (*Silence. Step forward.*) Forgive me. (*Silence. Step forward. Estragon lays his hand on Vladimir's shoulder.*) Come, Didi. (*Silence.*) Give me your hand. (*Vladimir half turns.*) Embrace me! (*Vladimir stiffens.*) Don't be stubborn! (*Vladimir softens. They embrace. Estragon recoils.*) You stink of garlic!

VLADIMIR: It's for the kidneys. (*Silence. Estragon looks attentively at the tree.*) What do we do now?

ESTRAGON: Wait.

VLADIMIR: Yes, but while waiting.

ESTRAGON: What about hanging ourselves?

VLADIMIR: Hmm. It'd give us an erection.

ESTRAGON: (*highly excited*). An erection!

VLADIMIR: With all that follows. Where it falls mandrakes grow. That's why they shriek when you pull them up. Did you not know that?

ESTRAGON: Let's hang ourselves immediately!

VLADIMIR: From a bough? (*They go towards the tree.*) I wouldn't trust it.

ESTRAGON: We can always try.

VLADIMIR: Go ahead.

ESTRAGON: After you.

VLADIMIR: No no, you first.

ESTRAGON: Why me?

VLADIMIR: You're lighter than I am.

ESTRAGON: Just so!

VLADIMIR: I don't understand.

ESTRAGON: Use your intelligence, can't you?
Vladimir uses his intelligence.

VLADIMIR: (*finally*). I remain in the dark.

ESTRAGON: This is how it is. (*He reflects.*) The bough . . .
the bough . . . (*Angrily.*) Use your head, can't
you?

VLADIMIR: You're my only hope.

ESTRAGON: (*with effort*). Gogo light—bough not break—Gogo
dead. Didi heavy—bough break—Didi alone.
Whereas—

VLADIMIR: I hadn't thought of that.

ESTRAGON: If it hangs you it'll hang anything.

VLADIMIR: But am I heavier than you?

ESTRAGON: So you tell me. I don't know. There's an even
chance. Or nearly.

VLADIMIR: Well? What do we do?

ESTRAGON: Don't let's do anything. It's safer.

VLADIMIR: Let's wait and see what he says.

ESTRAGON: Who?

VLADIMIR: Godot.

ESTRAGON: Good idea.

VLADIMIR: Let's wait till we know exactly how we stand.

ESTRAGON: On the other hand it might be better to strike the
iron before it freezes.

VLADIMIR: I'm curious to hear what he has to offer. Then
we'll take it or leave it.

ESTRAGON: What exactly did we ask him for?

VLADIMIR: Were you not there?

ESTRAGON: I can't have been listening.

VLADIMIR: Oh . . . Nothing very definite.

ESTRAGON: A kind of prayer.

VLADIMIR: Precisely.

ESTRAGON: A vague supplication.

VLADIMIR: Exactly.

ESTRAGON: And what did he reply?

VLADIMIR: That he'd see.

ESTRAGON: That he couldn't promise anything.

VLADIMIR: That he'd have to think it over.

ESTRAGON: In the quiet of his home.

VLADIMIR: Consult his family.

ESTRAGON: His friends.

VLADIMIR: His agents.

ESTRAGON: His correspondents.

VLADIMIR: His books.

ESTRAGON: His bank account.

VLADIMIR: Before taking a decision.

ESTRAGON: It's the normal thing.

VLADIMIR: Is it not?

ESTRAGON: I think it is.

VLADIMIR: I think so too.

Silence.

ESTRAGON: (*anxious*). And we?

VLADIMIR: I beg your pardon?

ESTRAGON: I said, And we?

VLADIMIR: I don't understand.

ESTRAGON: Where do we come in?

13

VLADIMIR: Come in?

ESTRAGON: Take your time.

VLADIMIR: Come in? On our hands and knees.

ESTRAGON: As bad as that?

VLADIMIR: Your Worship wishes to assert his prerogatives?

ESTRAGON: We've no rights any more?

Laugh of Vladimir, stifled as before, less the smile.

VLADIMIR: You'd make me laugh if it wasn't prohibited.

ESTRAGON: We've lost our rights?

VLADIMIR: (*distinctly*). We got rid of them.

Silence. They remain motionless, arms dangling, heads sunk, sagging at the knees.

ESTRAGON: (*feebly*). We're not tied? (*Pause.*) We're not—

VLADIMIR: Listen!

They listen, grotesquely rigid.

ESTRAGON: I hear nothing.

VLADIMIR: Hsst! (*They listen. Estragon loses his balance, almost falls. He clutches the arm of Vladimir who totters. They listen, huddled together.*) Nor I.

Sighs of relief. They relax and separate.

ESTRAGON: You gave me a fright.

VLADIMIR: I thought it was he.

ESTRAGON: Who?

VLADIMIR: Godot.

ESTRAGON: Pah! The wind in the reeds.

VLADIMIR: I could have sworn I heard shouts.

ESTRAGON: And why would he shout?

VLADIMIR: At his horse.

Silence.

ESTRAGON: (*violently*). I'm hungry!

VLADIMIR: Do you want a carrot?

ESTRAGON: Is that all there is?

VLADIMIR: I might have some turnips.

ESTRAGON: Give me a carrot. (*Vladimir rummages in his pockets, takes out a turnip and gives it to Estragon who takes a bite out of it. Angrily.*) It's a turnip!

VLADIMIR: Oh pardon! I could have sworn it was a carrot. (*He rummages again in his pockets, finds nothing but turnips.*) All that's turnips. (*He rummages.*) You must have eaten the last. (*He rummages.*) Wait, I have it. (*He brings out a carrot and gives it to Estragon.*) There, dear fellow. (*Estragon wipes the carrot on his sleeve and begins to eat it.*) Make it last, that's the end of them.

ESTRAGON: (*chewing*). I asked you a question.

VLADIMIR: Ah.

ESTRAGON: Did you reply?

VLADIMIR: How's the carrot?

ESTRAGON: It's a carrot.

VLADIMIR: So much the better, so much the better. (*Pause.*) What was it you wanted to know?

ESTRAGON: I've forgotten. (*Chews.*) That's what annoys me. (*He looks at the carrot appreciatively, dangles it between finger and thumb.*) I'll never forget this carrot. (*He sucks the end of it meditatively.*) Ah yes, now I remember.

VLADIMIR: Well?

ESTRAGON: (*his mouth full, vacuously*). We're not tied?

VLADIMIR: I don't hear a word you're saying.

ESTRAGON: (*chews, swallows*). I'm asking you if we're tied.

VLADIMIR: Tied?

ESTRAGON: Ti-ed.

VLADIMIR: How do you mean tied?

ESTRAGON: Down.

VLADIMIR: But to whom? By whom?

ESTRAGON: To your man.

VLADIMIR: To Godot? Tied to Godot! What an idea! No question of it. (*Pause.*) For the moment.

ESTRAGON: His name is Godot?

VLADIMIR: I think so.

ESTRAGON: Fancy that. (*He raises what remains of the carrot by the stub of leaf, twirls it before his eyes.*) Funny, the more you eat the worse it gets.

VLADIMIR: With me it's just the opposite.

ESTRAGON: In other words?

VLADIMIR: I get used to the muck as I go along.

ESTRAGON: (*after prolonged reflection*). Is that the opposite?

VLADIMIR: Question of temperament.

ESTRAGON: Of character.

VLADIMIR: Nothing you can do about it.

ESTRAGON: No use struggling.

VLADIMIR: One is what one is.

ESTRAGON: No use wriggling.

VLADIMIR: The essential doesn't change.

ESTRAGON: Nothing to be done. (*He proffers the remains of the carrot to Vladimir.*) Like to finish it?
A terrible cry, close at hand. Estragon drops the carrot. They remain motionless, then together make a sudden rush towards the wings. Estragon

*stops halfway, runs back, picks up the carrot,
stuffs it in his pocket, runs to rejoin Vladimir who
is waiting for him, stops again, runs back, picks up
his boot, runs to rejoin Vladimir. Huddled
together, shoulders hunched, cringing away from
the menace, they wait.*

*Enter Pozzo and Lucky. Pozzo drives Lucky by
means of a rope passed round his neck, so that
Lucky is the first to enter, followed by the rope
which is long enough to let him reach the middle
of the stage before Pozzo appears. Lucky carries
a heavy bag, a folding stool, a picnic basket and a
greatcoat, Pozzo a whip.*

POZZO: *(off).* On! *(Crack of whip. Pozzo appears. They
cross the stage. Lucky passes before Vladimir and
Estragon and exit. Pozzo at the sight of Vladimir
and Estragon stops short. The rope tautens. Pozzo
jerks at it violently.)* Back!

*Noise of Lucky falling with all his baggage.
Vladimir and Estragon turn towards him, half
wishing half fearing to go to his assistance.
Vladimir takes a step towards Lucky, Estragon
holds him back by the sleeve.*

VLADIMIR: Let me go!

ESTRAGON: Stay where you are!

POZZO: Be careful! He's wicked. *(Vladimir and Estragon
turn towards Pozzo.)* With strangers.

ESTRAGON: *(undertone).* Is that him?

VLADIMIR: Who?

ESTRAGON: *(trying to remember the name).* Er . . .

15

VLADIMIR: Godot?

ESTRAGON: Yes.

POZZO: I present myself: Pozzo.

VLADIMIR: (*to Estragon*). Not at all!

ESTRAGON: He said Godot.

VLADIMIR: Not at all!

ESTRAGON: (*timidly, to Pozzo*). You're not Mr. Godot, Sir?

POZZO: (*terrifying voice*). I am Pozzo! (*Silence.*) Pozzo! (*Silence.*) Does that name mean nothing to you? (*Silence.*) I say does that name mean nothing to you?

Vladimir and Estragon look at each other questioningly.

ESTRAGON: (*pretending to search*). Bozzo . . . Bozzo . . .

VLADIMIR: (*ditto*). Pozzo . . . Pozzo . . .

POZZO: PPPOZZZO!

ESTRAGON: Ah! Pozzo . . . let me see . . . Pozzo . . .

VLADIMIR: Is it Pozzo or Bozzo?

ESTRAGON: Pozzo . . . no . . . I'm afraid I . . . no . . . I don't seem to . . .

Pozzo advances threateningly.

VLADIMIR: (*conciliating*). I once knew a family called Gozzo. The mother had the clap.

ESTRAGON: (*hastily*). We're not from these parts, Sir.

POZZO: (*halting*). You are human beings none the less. (*He puts on his glasses.*) As far as one can see. (*He takes off his glasses.*) Of the same species as myself. (*He bursts into an enormous laugh.*) Of the same species as Pozzo! Made in God's image!

VLADIMIR: Well you see—

POZZO: (*peremptory*). Who is Godot?

ESTRAGON: Godot?

POZZO: You took me for Godot.

VLADIMIR: Oh no, Sir, not for an instant, Sir.

POZZO: Who is he?

VLADIMIR: Oh he's a . . . he's a kind of acquaintance.

ESTRAGON: Nothing of the kind, we hardly know him.

VLADIMIR: True . . . we don't know him very well . . . but all the same . . .

ESTRAGON: Personally I wouldn't even know him if I saw him.

POZZO: You took me for him.

ESTRAGON: (*recoiling before Pozzo*). That's to say . . . you understand . . . the dusk . . . the strain . . . waiting . . . I confess . . . I imagined . . . for a second . . .

POZZO: Waiting? So you were waiting for him?

VLADIMIR: Well you see—

POZZO: Here? On my land?

VLADIMIR: We didn't intend any harm.

ESTRAGON: We meant well.

POZZO: The road is free to all.

VLADIMIR: That's how we looked at it.

POZZO: It's a disgrace. But there you are.

ESTRAGON: Nothing we can do about it.

POZZO: (*with magnanimous gesture*). Let's say no more about it. (*He jerks the rope.*) Up pig! (*Pause.*) Every time he drops he falls asleep. (*Jerks the rope.*) Up hog! (*Noise of Lucky getting up and picking up his baggage. Pozzo jerks the rope.*) Back! (*Enter Lucky backwards.*) Stop! (*Lucky stops.*) Turn! (*Lucky turns. To Vladimir and Estragon, affably.*) Gentlemen, I am happy to have met you. (*Before their incredulous expression.*) Yes yes, sincerely happy. (*He jerks the rope.*) Closer! (*Lucky advances.*) Stop! (*Lucky stops.*) Yes, the road seems long when one journeys all alone for . . . (*he consults his watch*) . . . yes . . . (*he calculates*) . . . yes, six hours, that's right, six hours on end, and never a soul in sight. (*To Lucky.*) Coat! (*Lucky puts down the bag, advances, gives the coat, goes back to his place, takes up the bag.*) Hold that! (*Pozzo holds out the whip. Lucky advances and, both his hands being occupied, takes the whip in his mouth, then goes back to his place. Pozzo begins to put on his coat, stops.*) Coat! (*Lucky puts down bag, basket and stool, advances, helps Pozzo on with his coat, goes back to his place and takes up bag, basket and stool.*) Touch of autumn in the air this evening. (*Pozzo finishes buttoning his coat, stoops, inspects himself, straightens up.*) Whip! (*Lucky advances, stoops, Pozzo snatches the whip from his mouth, Lucky goes back to his place.*) Yes, gentlemen, I cannot go for long without the society of my likes (*he puts on his glasses and looks at the two likes*) even when the likeness is an imperfect one. (*He takes off his glasses.*) Stool! (*Lucky puts down bag and basket, advances, opens stool, puts it down, goes back to his place, takes up bag and basket.*) Closer! (*Lucky puts down bag and basket,*

advances, moves stool, goes back to his place,
takes up bag and basket. Pozzo sits down, places
the butt of his whip against Lucky's chest and
pushes.) Back! (*Lucky takes a step back.*) Further!
(*Lucky takes another step back.*) Stop! (*Lucky*
stops. To Vladimir and Estragon.) That is why,
with your permission, I propose to dally with you
a moment, before I venture any further. Basket!
(*Lucky advances, gives the basket, goes back to*
his place.) The fresh air stimulates the jaded
appetite. (*He opens the basket, takes out a piece*
of chicken and a bottle of wine.) Basket! (*Lucky*
advances, picks up the basket and goes back to his
place.) Further! (*Lucky takes a step back.*) He
stinks. Happy days!
He drinks from the bottle, puts it down and
begins to eat. Silence. Vladimir and Estragon,
cautiously at first, then more boldly, begin to
circle about Lucky, inspecting him up and down.
Pozzo eats his chicken voraciously, throwing
away the bones after having sucked them. Lucky
sags slowly, until bag and basket touch the
ground, then straightens up with a start and
begins to sag again. Rhythm of one sleeping on
his feet.

ESTRAGON: What ails him?
VLADIMIR: He looks tired.
ESTRAGON: Why doesn't he put down his bags?
VLADIMIR: How do I know? (*They close in on him.*) Careful!
ESTRAGON: Say something to him.

17

VLADIMIR:	Look!
ESTRAGON:	What?
VLADIMIR:	*(pointing).* His neck!
ESTRAGON:	*(looking at the neck).* I see nothing.
VLADIMIR:	Here.

Estragon goes over beside Vladimir.

ESTRAGON:	Oh I say!
VLADIMIR:	A running sore!
ESTRAGON:	It's the rope.
VLADIMIR:	It's the rubbing.
ESTRAGON:	It's inevitable.
VLADIMIR:	It's the knot.
ESTRAGON:	It's the chafing.

They resume their inspection, dwell on the face.

VLADIMIR:	*(grudgingly).* He's not bad looking.
ESTRAGON:	*(shrugging his shoulders, wry face).* Would you say so?
VLADIMIR:	A trifle effeminate.
ESTRAGON:	Look at the slobber.
VLADIMIR:	It's inevitable.
ESTRAGON:	Look at the slaver.
VLADIMIR:	Perhaps he's a halfwit.
ESTRAGON:	A cretin.
VLADIMIR:	*(looking closer).* Looks like a goiter.
ESTRAGON:	*(ditto).* It's not certain.
VLADIMIR:	He's panting.
ESTRAGON:	It's inevitable.
VLADIMIR:	And his eyes!
ESTRAGON:	What about them?
VLADIMIR:	Goggling out of his head.

ESTRAGON: Looks at his last gasp to me.

VLADIMIR: It's not certain. (*Pause.*) Ask him a question.

ESTRAGON: Would that be a good thing?

VLADIMIR: What do we risk?

ESTRAGON: (*timidly*). Mister . . .

VLADIMIR: Louder.

ESTRAGON: (*louder*). Mister . . .

POZZO: Leave him in peace! (*They turn towards Pozzo who, having finished eating, wipes his mouth with the back of his hand.*) Can't you see he wants to rest? Basket! (*He strikes a match and begins to light his pipe. Estragon sees the chicken bones on the ground and stares at them greedily. As Lucky does not move Pozzo throws the match angrily away and jerks the rope.*) Basket! (*Lucky starts, almost falls, recovers his senses, advances, puts the bottle in the basket and goes back to his place. Estragon stares at the bones. Pozzo strikes another match and lights his pipe.*) What can you expect, it's not his job. (*He pulls at his pipe, stretches out his legs.*) Ah! That's better.

ESTRAGON: (*timidly*). Please Sir . . .

POZZO: What is it, my good man?

ESTRAGON: Er . . . you've finished with the . . . er . . . you don't need the . . . er . . . bones, Sir?

VLADIMIR: (*scandalized*). You couldn't have waited?

POZZO: No no, he does well to ask. Do I need the bones? (*He turns them over with the end of his whip.*) No, personally I do not need them any more. (*Estragon takes a step towards the bones.*) But

... (*Estragon stops short*) ... but in theory the bones go to the carrier. He is therefore the one to ask. (*Estragon turns towards Lucky, hesitates.*) Go on, go on, don't be afraid, ask him, he'll tell you.
Estragon goes towards Lucky, stops before him.

ESTRAGON: Mister ... excuse me, Mister ...

POZZO: You're being spoken to, pig! Reply! (*To Estragon.*) Try him again.

ESTRAGON: Excuse me, Mister, the bones, you won't be wanting the bones?
Lucky looks long at Estragon.

POZZO: (*in raptures*). Mister! (*Lucky bows his head.*) Reply! Do you want them or don't you? (*Silence of Lucky. To Estragon.*) They're yours. (*Estragon makes a dart at the bones, picks them up and begins to gnaw them.*) I don't like it. I've never known him refuse a bone before. (*He looks anxiously at Lucky.*) Nice business it'd be if he fell sick on me!
He puffs at his pipe.

VLADIMIR: (*exploding*). It's a scandal!
Silence. Flabbergasted, Estragon stops gnawing, looks at Pozzo and Vladimir in turn. Pozzo outwardly calm. Vladimir embarrassed.

POZZO: (*to Vladimir*). Are you alluding to anything in particular?

VLADIMIR: (*stutteringly resolute*). To treat a man ... (*gesture towards Lucky*) ... like that ... I think that ... no ... a human being ... no ... it's a scandal!

ESTRAGON: (*not to be outdone*). A disgrace!
He resumes his gnawing.

POZZO: You are severe. (*To Vladimir.*) What age are you, if it's not a rude question? (*Silence.*) Sixty? Seventy? (*To Estragon.*) What age would you say he was?

ESTRAGON: Eleven.

POZZO: I am impertinent. (*He knocks out his pipe against the whip, gets up.*) I must be getting on. Thank you for your society. (*He reflects.*) Unless I smoke another pipe before I go. What do you say? (*They say nothing.*) Oh I'm only a small smoker, a very small smoker, I'm not in the habit of smoking two pipes one on top of the other, it makes (*hand to heart, sighing*) my heart go pit-a-pat. (*Silence.*) It's the nicotine, one absorbs it in spite of one's precautions. (*Sighs.*) You know how it is. (*Silence.*) But perhaps you don't smoke? Yes? No? It's of no importance. (*Silence.*) But how am I to sit down now, without affectation, now that I have risen? Without appearing to—how shall I say—without appearing to falter. (*To Vladimir.*) I beg your pardon? (*Silence.*) Perhaps you didn't speak? (*Silence.*) It's of no importance. Let me see . . .
He reflects.

ESTRAGON: Ah! That's better.
He puts the bones in his pocket.

VLADIMIR: Let's go.

ESTRAGON: So soon?

POZZO: One moment! (*He jerks the rope.*) Stool! (*He points with his whip. Lucky moves the stool.*) More! There! (*He sits down. Lucky goes back to his place.*) Done it!
He fills his pipe.

VLADIMIR: (*vehemently*). Let's go!

POZZO: I hope I'm not driving you away. Wait a little longer, you'll never regret it.

ESTRAGON: (*scenting charity*). We're in no hurry.

POZZO: (*having lit his pipe*). The second is never so sweet . . . (*he takes the pipe out of his mouth, contemplates it*) . . . as the first I mean. (*He puts the pipe back in his mouth.*) But it's sweet just the same.

VLADIMIR: I'm going.

POZZO: He can no longer endure my presence. I am perhaps not particularly human, but who cares? (*To Vladimir.*) Think twice before you do anything rash. Suppose you go now while it is still day, for there is no denying it is still day. (*They all look up at the sky.*) Good. (*They stop looking at the sky.*) What happens in that case—(*he takes the pipe out of his mouth, examines it*)—I'm out—(*he relights his pipe*)—in that case—(*puff*)—in that case—(*puff*) —what happens in that case to your appointment with this . . . Godet . . . Godot . . . Godin . . . anyhow you see who I mean, who has your future in his hands . . . (*pause*) . . . at least your immediate future?

VLADIMIR: Who told you?

POZZO: He speaks to me again! If this goes on much longer we'll soon be old friends.

ESTRAGON: Why doesn't he put down his bags?

POZZO: I too would be happy to meet him. The more people I meet the happier I become. From the meanest creature one departs wiser, richer, more conscious of one's blessings. Even you . . . (*he looks at them ostentatiously in turn to make it clear they are both meant*) . . . even you, who knows, will have added to my store.

ESTRAGON: Why doesn't he put down his bags?

POZZO: But that would surprise me.

VLADIMIR: You're being asked a question.

POZZO: (*delighted*). A question! Who? What? A moment ago you were calling me Sir, in fear and trembling. Now you're asking me questions. No good will come of this!

VLADIMIR: (*to Estragon*). I think he's listening.

ESTRAGON: (*circling about Lucky*). What?

VLADIMIR: You can ask him now. He's on the alert.

ESTRAGON: Ask him what?

VLADIMIR: Why he doesn't put down his bags.

ESTRAGON: I wonder.

VLADIMIR: Ask him, can't you?

POZZO: (*who has followed these exchanges with anxious attention, fearing lest the question get lost*). You want to know why he doesn't put down his bags, as you call them.

VLADIMIR: That's it.

20

POZZO: *(to Estragon).* You are sure you agree with that?

ESTRAGON: He's puffing like a grampus.

POZZO: The answer is this. *(To Estragon.)* But stay still, I beg of you, you're making me nervous!

VLADIMIR: Here.

ESTRAGON: What is it?

VLADIMIR: He's about to speak.

Estragon goes over beside Vladimir. Motionless, side by side, they wait.

POZZO: Good. Is everybody ready? Is everybody looking at me? *(He looks at Lucky, jerks the rope. Lucky raises his head.)* Will you look at me, pig! *(Lucky looks at him.)* Good. *(He puts the pipe in his pocket, takes out a little vaporizer and sprays his throat, puts back the vaporizer in his pocket, clears his throat, spits, takes out the vaporizer again, sprays his throat again, puts back the vaporizer in his pocket.)* I am ready. Is everybody listening? Is everybody ready? *(He looks at them all in turn, jerks the rope.)* Hog! *(Lucky raises his head.)* I don't like talking in a vacuum. Good. Let me see.

He reflects.

ESTRAGON: I'm going.

POZZO: What was it exactly you wanted to know?

VLADIMIR: Why he—

POZZO: *(angrily).* Don't interrupt me! *(Pause. Calmer.)* If we all speak at once we'll never get anywhere. *(Pause.)* What was I saying? *(Pause. Louder.)* What was I saying?

Vladimir mimics one carrying a heavy burden.
Pozzo looks at him, puzzled.

ESTRAGON: (*forcibly*). Bags. (*He points at Lucky.*) Why?
Always hold. (*He sags, panting.*) Never put down.
(*He opens his hands, straightens up with relief.*)
Why?

POZZO: Ah! Why couldn't you say so before? Why he
doesn't make himself comfortable? Let's try and
get this clear. Has he not the right to? Certainly
he has. It follows that he doesn't want to. There's
reasoning for you. And why doesn't he want to?
(*Pause.*) Gentlemen, the reason is this.

VLADIMIR: (*to Estragon*). Make a note of this.

POZZO: He wants to impress me, so that I'll keep him.

ESTRAGON: What?

POZZO: Perhaps I haven't got it quite right. He wants to
mollify me, so that I'll give up the idea of parting
with him. No, that's not exactly it either.

VLADIMIR: You want to get rid of him?

POZZO: He wants to cod me, but he won't.

VLADIMIR: You want to get rid of him?

POZZO: He imagines that when I see how well he carries
I'll be tempted to keep him on in that capacity.

ESTRAGON: You've had enough of him?

POZZO: In reality he carries like a pig. It's not his job.

VLADIMIR: You want to get rid of him?

POZZO: He imagines that when I see him indefatigable
I'll regret my decision. Such is his miserable
scheme. As though I were short of slaves! (*All
three look at Lucky.*) Atlas, son of Jupiter!

(*Silence.*) Well, that's that I think. Anything else?
Vaporizer.

VLADIMIR: You want to get rid of him?

POZZO: Remark that I might just as well have been in his
shoes and he in mine. If chance had not willed
otherwise. To each one his due.

VLADIMIR: You waagerrim?

POZZO: I beg your pardon?

VLADIMIR: You want to get rid of him?

POZZO: I do. But instead of driving him away as I might
have done, I mean instead of simply kicking him
out on his arse, in the goodness of my heart I am
bringing him to the fair, where I hope to get a
good price for him. The truth is you can't drive
such creatures away. The best thing would be to
kill them.
Lucky weeps.

ESTRAGON: He's crying!

POZZO: Old dogs have more dignity. (*He proffers his
handkerchief to Estragon.*) Comfort him, since
you pity him. (*Estragon hesitates.*) Come on.
(*Estragon takes the handkerchief.*) Wipe away his
tears, he'll feel less forsaken.
Estragon hesitates.

VLADIMIR: Here, give it to me, I'll do it.
Estragon refuses to give the handkerchief.
Childish gestures.

POZZO: Make haste, before he stops. (*Estragon approaches
Lucky and makes to wipe his eyes. Lucky kicks
him violently in the shins. Estragon drops the*

handkerchief, recoils, staggers about the stage howling with pain.) Hanky!

Lucky puts down bag and basket, picks up handkerchief and gives it to Pozzo, goes back to his place, picks up bag and basket.

ESTRAGON: Oh the swine! (*He pulls up the leg of his trousers.*) He's crippled me!

POZZO: I told you he didn't like strangers.

VLADIMIR: (*to Estragon*). Show. (*Estragon shows his leg. To Pozzo, angrily.*) He's bleeding!

POZZO: It's a good sign.

ESTRAGON: (*on one leg*). I'll never walk again!

VLADIMIR: (*tenderly*). I'll carry you. (*Pause.*) If necessary.

POZZO: He's stopped crying. (*To Estragon.*) You have replaced him as it were. (*Lyrically.*) The tears of the world are a constant quantity. For each one who begins to weep somewhere else another stops. The same is true of the laugh. (*He laughs.*) Let us not then speak ill of our generation, it is not any unhappier than its predecessors. (*Pause.*) Let us not speak well of it either. (*Pause.*) Let us not speak of it at all. (*Pause. Judiciously.*) It is true the population has increased.

VLADIMIR: Try and walk.

Estragon takes a few limping steps, stops before Lucky and spits on him, then goes and sits down on the mound.

POZZO: Guess who taught me all these beautiful things. (*Pause. Pointing to Lucky.*) My Lucky!

22

VLADIMIR: (*looking at the sky*). Will night never come?

POZZO: But for him all my thoughts, all my feelings, would have been of common things. (*Pause. With extraordinary vehemence.*) Professional worries! (*Calmer.*) Beauty, grace, truth of the first water, I knew they were all beyond me. So I took a knook.

VLADIMIR: (*startled from his inspection of the sky*). A knook?

POZZO: That was nearly sixty years ago . . . (*he consults his watch*) . . . yes, nearly sixty. (*Drawing himself up proudly.*) You wouldn't think it to look at me, would you? Compared to him I look like a young man, no? (*Pause.*) Hat! (*Lucky puts down the basket and takes off his hat. His long white hair falls about his face. He puts his hat under his arm and picks up the basket.*) Now look. (*Pozzo takes off his hat.[1] He is completely bald. He puts on his hat again.*) Did you see?

VLADIMIR: And now you turn him away? Such an old and faithful servant!

ESTRAGON: Swine!

Pozzo more and more agitated.

VLADIMIR: After having sucked all the good out of him you chuck him away like a . . . like a banana skin. Really . . .

POZZO: (*groaning, clutching his head*). I can't bear it . . . any longer . . . the way he goes on . . . you've no idea . . . it's terrible . . . he must go . . . (*he waves his arms*) . . . I'm going mad . . . (*he

[1] All four wear bowlers.

collapses, his head in his hands) . . . I can't bear
it . . . any longer . . .
Silence. All look at Pozzo.

VLADIMIR: He can't bear it.

ESTRAGON: Any longer.

VLADIMIR: He's going mad.

ESTRAGON: It's terrible.

VLADIMIR: (*to Lucky*). How dare you! It's abominable! Such a
good master! Crucify him like that! After so many
years! Really!

POZZO: (*sobbing*). He used to be so kind . . . so helpful
. . . and entertaining . . . my good angel . . .
and now . . . he's killing me

ESTRAGON: (*to Vladimir*). Does he want to replace him?

VLADIMIR: What?

ESTRAGON: Does he want someone to take his place or not?

VLADIMIR: I don't think so.

ESTRAGON: What?

VLADIMIR: I don't know.

ESTRAGON: Ask him.

POZZO: (*calmer*). Gentlemen, I don't know what came over
me. Forgive me. Forget all I said. (*More and more
his old self.*) I don't remember exactly what it was,
but you may be sure there wasn't a word of truth
in it. (*Drawing himself up, striking his chest.*) Do
I look like a man that can be made to suffer?
Frankly? (*He rummages in his pockets.*) What
have I done with my pipe?

VLADIMIR: Charming evening we're having.

ESTRAGON: Unforgettable.

23

VLADIMIR: And it's not over.

ESTRAGON: Apparently not.

VLADIMIR: It's only beginning.

ESTRAGON: It's awful.

VLADIMIR: Worse than the pantomime.

ESTRAGON: The circus.

VLADIMIR: The music-hall.

ESTRAGON: The circus.

POZZO: What can I have done with that briar?

ESTRAGON: He's a scream. He's lost his dudeen.
Laughs noisily.

VLADIMIR: I'll be back.
He hastens towards the wings.

ESTRAGON: End of the corridor, on the left.

VLADIMIR: Keep my seat.
Exit Vladimir.

POZZO: (*on the point of tears*). I've lost my Kapp and
Peterson!

ESTRAGON: (*convulsed with merriment*). He'll be the death of
me!

POZZO: You didn't see by any chance—. (*He misses
Vladimir.*) Oh! He's gone! Without saying
goodbye! How could he! He might have waited!

ESTRAGON: He would have burst.

POZZO: Oh! (*Pause.*) Oh well then of course in that
case . . .

ESTRAGON: Come here.

POZZO: What for?

ESTRAGON: You'll see.

POZZO: You want me to get up?

ESTRAGON: Quick! (*Pozzo gets up and goes over beside Estragon. Estragon points off.*) Look!

POZZO: (*having put on his glasses*). Oh I say!

ESTRAGON: It's all over.

Enter Vladimir, somber. He shoulders Lucky out of his way, kicks over the stool, comes and goes agitatedly.

POZZO: He's not pleased.

ESTRAGON: (*to Vladimir*). You missed a treat. Pity.

Vladimir halts, straightens the stool, comes and goes, calmer.

POZZO: He subsides. (*Looking round.*) Indeed all subsides. A great calm descends. (*Raising his hand.*) Listen! Pan sleeps.

VLADIMIR: Will night never come?

All three look at the sky.

POZZO: You don't feel like going until it does?

ESTRAGON: Well you see—

POZZO: Why it's very natural, very natural. I myself in your situation, if I had an appointment with a Godin . . . Godet . . . Godot . . . anyhow you see who I mean, I'd wait till it was black night before I gave up. (*He looks at the stool.*) I'd very much like to sit down, but I don't quite know how to go about it.

ESTRAGON: Could I be of any help?

POZZO: If you asked me perhaps.

ESTRAGON: What?

POZZO: If you asked me to sit down.

ESTRAGON: Would that be a help?

POZZO: I fancy so.

ESTRAGON: Here we go. Be seated, Sir, I beg of you.

POZZO: No no, I wouldn't think of it! (*Pause. Aside.*) Ask me again.

ESTRAGON: Come come, take a seat I beseech you, you'll get pneumonia.

POZZO: You really think so?

ESTRAGON: Why it's absolutely certain.

POZZO: No doubt you are right. (*He sits down.*) Done it again! (*Pause.*) Thank you, dear fellow. (*He consults his watch.*) But I must really be getting along, if I am to observe my schedule.

VLADIMIR: Time has stopped.

POZZO: (*cuddling his watch to his ear*). Don't you believe it, Sir, don't you believe it. (*He puts his watch back in his pocket.*) Whatever you like, but not that.

ESTRAGON: (*to Pozzo*). Everything seems black to him to-day.

POZZO: Except the firmament. (*He laughs, pleased with this witticism.*) But I see what it is, you are not from these parts, you don't know what our twilights can do. Shall I tell you? (*Silence. Estragon is fiddling with his boot again, Vladimir with his hat.*) I can't refuse you. (*Vaporizer.*) A little attention, if you please. (*Vladimir and Estragon continue their fiddling, Lucky is half asleep. Pozzo cracks his whip feebly.*) What's the matter with this whip? (*He gets up and cracks it more vigorously, finally with success. Lucky jumps. Vladimir's hat, Estragon's boot, Lucky's* hat, fall to the ground. *Pozzo throws down the whip.*) Worn out, this whip. (*He looks at Vladimir and Estragon.*) What was I saying?

VLADIMIR: Let's go.

ESTRAGON: But take the weight off your feet, I implore you, you'll catch your death.

POZZO: True. (*He sits down. To Estragon.*) What is your name?

ESTRAGON: Adam.

POZZO: (*who hasn't listened*). Ah yes! The night. (*He raises his head.*) But be a little more attentive, for pity's sake, otherwise we'll never get anywhere. (*He looks at the sky.*) Look! (*All look at the sky except Lucky who is dozing off again. Pozzo jerks the rope.*) Will you look at the sky, pig! (*Lucky looks at the sky.*) Good, that's enough. (*They stop looking at the sky.*) What is there so extraordinary about it? Qua sky. It is pale and luminous like any sky at this hour of the day. (*Pause.*) In these latitudes. (*Pause.*) When the weather is fine. (*Lyrical.*) An hour ago (*he looks at his watch, prosaic*) roughly (*lyrical*) after having poured forth even since (*he hesitates, prosaic*) say ten o'clock in the morning (*lyrical*) tirelessly torrents of red and white light it begins to lose its effulgence, to grow pale (*gesture of the two hands lapsing by stages*) pale, ever a little paler, a little paler until (*dramatic pause, ample gesture of the two hands flung wide apart*) pppfff! finished! it comes to rest. But—(*hand raised in admonition*)—

25

but behind this veil of gentleness and peace night
is charging (*vibrantly*) and will burst upon us
(*snaps his fingers*) pop! like that! (*his inspiration
leaves him*) just when we least expect it. (*Silence.
Gloomily.*) That's how it is on this bitch of an
earth.

    Long silence.

ESTRAGON: So long as one knows.

VLADIMIR: One can bide one's time.

ESTRAGON: One knows what to expect.

VLADIMIR: No further need to worry.

ESTRAGON: Simply wait.

VLADIMIR: We're used to it.

    *He picks up his hat, peers inside it, shakes it, puts
    it on.*

POZZO: How did you find me? (*Vladimir and Estragon
look at him blankly.*) Good? Fair? Middling?
Poor? Positively bad?

VLADIMIR: (*first to understand*). Oh very good, very very
good.

POZZO: (*to Estragon*). And you, Sir?

ESTRAGON: Oh tray bong, tray tray tray bong.

POZZO: (*fervently*). Bless you, gentlemen, bless you!
(*Pause.*) I have such need of encouragement!
(*Pause.*) I weakened a little towards the end, you
didn't notice?

VLADIMIR: Oh perhaps just a teeny weeny little bit.

ESTRAGON: I thought it was intentional.

POZZO: You see my memory is defective.

    Silence.

ESTRAGON: In the meantime nothing happens.

POZZO: You find it tedious?

ESTRAGON: Somewhat.

POZZO: (*to Vladimir*). And you, Sir?

VLADIMIR: I've been better entertained.
Silence. Pozzo struggles inwardly.

POZZO: Gentlemen, you have been . . . civil to me.

ESTRAGON: Not at all!

VLADIMIR: What an idea!

POZZO: Yes yes, you have been correct. So that I ask myself is there anything I can do in my turn for these honest fellows who are having such a dull, dull time.

ESTRAGON: Even ten francs would be a help.

VLADIMIR: We are not beggars!

POZZO: Is there anything I can do, that's what I ask myself, to cheer them up? I have given them bones, I have talked to them about this and that, I have explained the twilight, admittedly. But is it enough, that's what tortures me, is it enough?

ESTRAGON: Even five.

VLADIMIR: (*to Estragon, indignantly*). That's enough!

ESTRAGON: I couldn't accept less.

POZZO: Is it enough? No doubt. But I am liberal. It's my nature. This evening. So much the worse for me. (*He jerks the rope. Lucky looks at him.*) For I shall suffer, no doubt about that. (*He picks up the whip.*) What do you prefer? Shall we have him dance, or sing, or recite, or think, or—

ESTRAGON: Who?

POZZO: Who! You know how to think, you two?

VLADIMIR: He thinks?

POZZO: Certainly. Aloud. He even used to think very prettily once, I could listen to him for hours. Now . . . (*he shudders*). So much the worse for me. Well, would you like him to think something for us?

ESTRAGON: I'd rather he'd dance, it'd be more fun.

POZZO: Not necessarily.

ESTRAGON: Wouldn't it, Didi, be more fun?

VLADIMIR: I'd like well to hear him think.

ESTRAGON: Perhaps he could dance first and think afterwards, if it isn't too much to ask him.

VLADIMIR: (*to Pozzo*). Would that be possible?

POZZO: By all means, nothing simpler. It's the natural order.
He laughs briefly.

VLADIMIR: Then let him dance.
Silence.

POZZO: Do you hear, hog?

ESTRAGON: He never refuses?

POZZO: He refused once. (*Silence.*) Dance, misery!
Lucky puts down bag and basket, advances towards front, turns to Pozzo. Lucky dances. He stops.

ESTRAGON: Is that all?

POZZO: Encore!
Lucky executes the same movements, stops.

ESTRAGON: Pooh! I'd do as well myself. (*He imitates Lucky, almost falls.*) With a little practice.

POZZO: He used to dance the farandole, the fling, the brawl, the jig, the fandango and even the hornpipe. He capered. For joy. Now that's the best he can do. Do you know what he calls it?

ESTRAGON: The Scapegoat's Agony.

VLADIMIR: The Hard Stool.

POZZO: The Net. He thinks he's entangled in a net.

VLADIMIR: (*squirming like an aesthete*). There's something about it . . .
Lucky makes to return to his burdens.

POZZO: Woaa!
Lucky stiffens.

ESTRAGON: Tell us about the time he refused.

POZZO: With pleasure, with pleasure. (*He fumbles in his pockets.*) Wait. (*He fumbles.*) What have I done with my spray? (*He fumbles.*) Well now isn't that . . . (*He looks up, consternation on his features. Faintly.*) I can't find my pulverizer!

ESTRAGON: (*faintly*). My left lung is very weak! (*He coughs feebly. In ringing tones.*) But my right lung is as sound as a bell!

POZZO: (*normal voice*). No matter! What was I saying. (*He ponders.*) Wait. (*Ponders.*) Well now isn't that . . . (*He raises his head.*) Help me!

ESTRAGON: Wait!

VLADIMIR: Wait!

POZZO: Wait!
All three take off their hats simultaneously, press their hands to their foreheads, concentrate.

ESTRAGON: (*triumphantly*). Ah!

27

VLADIMIR:	He has it.
POZZO:	*(impatient)*. Well?
ESTRAGON:	Why doesn't he put down his bags?
VLADIMIR:	Rubbish!
POZZO:	Are you sure?
VLADIMIR:	Damn it haven't you already told us?
POZZO:	I've already told you?
ESTRAGON:	He's already told us?
VLADIMIR:	Anyway he has put them down.
ESTRAGON:	*(glance at Lucky)*. So he has. And what of it?
VLADIMIR:	Since he has put down his bags it is impossible we should have asked why he does not do so.
POZZO:	Stoutly reasoned!
ESTRAGON:	And why has he put them down?
POZZO:	Answer us that.
VLADIMIR:	In order to dance.
ESTRAGON:	True!
POZZO:	True!
	Silence. They put on their hats.
ESTRAGON:	Nothing happens, nobody comes, nobody goes, it's awful!
VLADIMIR:	*(to Pozzo)*. Tell him to think.
POZZO:	Give him his hat.
VLADIMIR:	His hat?
POZZO:	He can't think without his hat.
VLADIMIR:	*(to Estragon)*. Give him his hat.
ESTRAGON:	Me! After what he did to me! Never!
VLADIMIR:	I'll give it to him.
	He does not move.
ESTRAGON:	*(to Pozzo)*. Tell him to go and fetch it.

POZZO: It's better to give it to him.

VLADIMIR: I'll give it to him.

He picks up the hat and tenders it at arm's length to Lucky, who does not move.

POZZO: You must put it on his head.

ESTRAGON: *(to Pozzo).* Tell him to take it.

POZZO: It's better to put it on his head.

VLADIMIR: I'll put it on his head.

He goes round behind Lucky, approaches him cautiously, puts the hat on his head and recoils smartly. Lucky does not move. Silence.

ESTRAGON: What's he waiting for?

POZZO: Stand back! *(Vladimir and Estragon move away from Lucky. Pozzo jerks the rope. Lucky looks at Pozzo.)* Think, pig! *(Pause. Lucky begins to dance.)* Stop! *(Lucky stops.)* Forward! *(Lucky advances.)* Stop! *(Lucky stops.)* Think!
Silence.

LUCKY: On the other hand with regard to—

POZZO: Stop! *(Lucky stops.)* Back! *(Lucky moves back.)* Stop! *(Lucky stops.)* Turn! *(Lucky turns towards auditorium.)* Think!
During Lucky's tirade the others react as follows.
1) Vladimir and Estragon all attention, Pozzo dejected and disgusted.
2) Vladimir and Estragon begin to protest, Pozzo's sufferings increase.
3) Vladimir and Estragon attentive again, Pozzo more and more agitated and groaning.
4) Vladimir and Estragon protest violently. Pozzo

jumps up, pulls on the rope. General outcry.
Lucky pulls on the rope, staggers, shouts his text.
All three throw themselves on Lucky who
struggles and shouts his text.

LUCKY: Given the existence as uttered forth in the public
works of Puncher and Wattmann of a personal
God quaquaquaqua with white beard
quaquaquaqua outside time without extension
who from the heights of divine apathia divine
athambia divine aphasia loves us dearly with
some exceptions for reasons unknown but time
will tell and suffers like the divine Miranda with
those who for reasons unknown but time will tell
are plunged in torment plunged in fire whose fire
flames if that continues and who can doubt it will
fire the firmament that is to say blast hell to
heaven so blue still and calm so calm with a calm
which even though intermittent is better than
nothing but not so fast and considering what is
more that as a result of the labors left unfinished
crowned by the Acacacacademy of
Anthropopopometry of Essy-in-Possy of Testew
and Cunard it is established beyond all doubt all
other doubt than that which clings to the labors
of men that as a result of the labors unfinished of
Testew and Cunard it is established as hereinafter
but not so fast for reasons unknown that as a
result of the public works of Puncher and
Wattmann it is established beyond all doubt that
in view of the labors of Fartov and Belcher left

unfinished for reasons unknown of Testew and
Cunard left unfinished it is established what many
deny that man in Possy of Testew and Cunard
that man in Essy that man in short that man in
brief in spite of the strides of alimentation and
defecation wastes and pines wastes and pines and
concurrently simultaneously what is more for
reasons unknown in spite of the strides of physical
culture the practice of sports such as tennis
football running cycling swimming flying floating
riding gliding conating camogie skating tennis of
all kinds dying flying sports of all sorts autumn
summer winter winter tennis of all kinds hockey of
all sorts penicilline and succedanea in a word I
resume flying gliding golf over nine and eighteen
holes tennis of all sorts in a word for reasons
unknown in Feckham Peckham Fulham Clapham
namely concurrently simultaneously what is more
for reasons unknown but time will tell fades away
I resume Fulham Clapham in a word the dead
loss per head since the death of Bishop Berkeley
being to the tune of one inch four ounce per head
approximately by and large more or less to the
nearest decimal good measure round figures stark
naked in the stockinged feet in Connemara in a
word for reasons unknown no matter what matter
the facts are there and considering what is more
much more grave that in the light of the labors
lost of Steinweg and Peterman it appears what is
more much more grave that in the light the light

29

the light of the labors lost of Steinweg and
Peterman that in the plains in the mountains by
the seas by the rivers running water running fire
the air is the same and then the earth namely the
air and then the earth in the great cold the great
dark the air and the earth abode of stones in the
great cold alas alas in the year of their Lord six
hundred and something the air the earth the sea
the earth abode of stones in the great deeps the
great cold on sea on land and in the air I resume
for reasons unknown in spite of the tennis the
facts are there but time will tell I resume alas
alas on on in short in fine on on abode of stones
who can doubt it I resume but not so fast I
resume the skull fading fading fading and
concurrently simultaneously what is more for
reasons unknown in spite of the tennis on on the
beard the flames the tears the stones so blue so
calm alas alas on on the skull the skull the skull
the skull in Connemara in spite of the tennis the
labors abandoned left unfinished graver still
abode of stones in a word I resume alas alas
abandoned unfinished the skull the skull in
Connemara in spite of the tennis the skull alas the
stones Cunard (*mêlée, final vociferations*) tennis
. . . the stones . . . so calm . . . Cunard . . .
unfinished . . .

POZZO: His hat!

*Vladimir seizes Lucky's hat. Silence of Lucky. He
falls. Silence. Panting of the victors.*

ESTRAGON: Avenged!

Vladimir examines the hat, peers inside it.

POZZO: Give me that! (*He snatches the hat from Vladimir, throws it on the ground, tramples on it.*) There's an end to his thinking!

VLADIMIR: But will he be able to walk?

POZZO: Walk or crawl! (*He kicks Lucky.*) Up pig!

ESTRAGON: Perhaps he's dead.

VLADIMIR: You'll kill him.

POZZO: Up scum! (*He jerks the rope.*) Help me!

VLADIMIR: How?

POZZO: Raise him up!

Vladimir and Estragon hoist Lucky to his feet, support him an instant, then let him go. He falls.

ESTRAGON: He's doing it on purpose!

POZZO: You must hold him. (*Pause.*) Come on, come on, raise him up.

ESTRAGON: To hell with him!

VLADIMIR: Come on, once more.

ESTRAGON: What does he take us for?

They raise Lucky, hold him up.

POZZO: Don't let him go! (*Vladimir and Estragon totter.*) Don't move! (*Pozzo fetches bag and basket and brings them towards Lucky.*) Hold him tight! (*He puts the bag in Lucky's hand. Lucky drops it immediately.*) Don't let him go! (*He puts back the bag in Lucky's hand. Gradually, at the feel of the bag, Lucky recovers his senses and his fingers finally close round the handle.*) Hold him tight! (*As before with basket.*) Now! You can let him go.

(Vladimir and Estragon move away from Lucky who totters, reels, sags, but succeeds in remaining on his feet, bag and basket in his hands. Pozzo steps back, cracks his whip.) Forward! *(Lucky totters forward.)* Back! *(Lucky totters back.)* Turn! *(Lucky turns.)* Done it! He can walk. *(Turning to Vladimir and Estragon.)* Thank you, gentlemen, and let me . . . *(he fumbles in his pockets)* . . . let me wish you . . . *(fumbles)* . . . wish you . . . *(fumbles)* . . . what have I done with my watch? *(Fumbles.)* A genuine half-hunter, gentlemen, with deadbeat escapement! *(Sobbing.)* Twas my granpa gave it to me! *(He searches on the ground, Vladimir and Estragon likewise. Pozzo turns over with his foot the remains of Lucky's hat.)* Well now isn't that just—

VLADIMIR: Perhaps it's in your fob.

POZZO: Wait! *(He doubles up in an attempt to apply his ear to his stomach, listens. Silence.)* I hear nothing. *(He beckons them to approach. Vladimir and Estragon go over to him, bend over his stomach.)* Surely one should hear the tick-tick.

VLADIMIR: Silence!

All listen, bent double.

ESTRAGON: I hear something.

POZZO: Where?

VLADIMIR: It's the heart.

POZZO: *(disappointed).* Damnation!

VLADIMIR: Silence!

ESTRAGON: Perhaps it has stopped.

They straighten up.

POZZO: Which of you smells so bad?

ESTRAGON: He has stinking breath and I have stinking feet.

POZZO: I must go.

ESTRAGON: And your half-hunter?

POZZO: I must have left it at the manor.

Silence.

ESTRAGON: Then adieu.

POZZO: Adieu.

VLADIMIR: Adieu.

POZZO: Adieu.

Silence. No one moves.

VLADIMIR: Adieu.

POZZO: Adieu.

ESTRAGON: Adieu.

Silence.

POZZO: And thank you.

VLADIMIR: Thank *you.*

POZZO: Not at all.

ESTRAGON: Yes yes.

POZZO: No no.

VLADIMIR: Yes yes.

ESTRAGON: No no.

Silence.

POZZO: I don't seem to be able . . . (*long hesitation*) . . . to depart.

ESTRAGON: Such is life.

Pozzo turns, moves away from Lucky towards the wings, paying out the rope as he goes.

VLADIMIR: You're going the wrong way.

POZZO: I need a running start. (*Having come to the end of the rope, i.e. off stage, he stops, turns and cries.*) Stand back! (*Vladimir and Estragon stand back, look towards Pozzo. Crack of whip.*) On! On!

ESTRAGON: On!

VLADIMIR: On!
Lucky moves off.

POZZO: Faster! (*He appears, crosses the stage preceded by Lucky. Vladimir and Estragon wave their hats. Exit Lucky.*) On! On! (*On the point of disappearing in his turn he stops and turns. The rope tautens. Noise of Lucky falling off.*) Stool! (*Vladimir fetches stool and gives it to Pozzo who throws it to Lucky.*) Adieu!

VLADIMIR:
ESTRAGON: (*waving*). Adieu! Adieu!

POZZO: Up! Pig! (*Noise of Lucky getting up.*) On! (*Exit Pozzo.*) Faster! On! Adieu! Pig! Yip! Adieu!
Long silence.

VLADIMIR: That passed the time.

ESTRAGON: It would have passed in any case.

VLADIMIR: Yes, but not so rapidly.
Pause.

ESTRAGON: What do we do now?

VLADIMIR: I don't know.

ESTRAGON: Let's go.

VLADIMIR: We can't.

ESTRAGON: Why not?

VLADIMIR: We're waiting for Godot.

ESTRAGON: (*despairingly*). Ah!
Pause.
VLADIMIR: How they've changed!
ESTRAGON: Who?
VLADIMIR: Those two.
ESTRAGON: That's the idea, let's make a little conversation.
VLADIMIR: Haven't they?
ESTRAGON: What?
VLADIMIR: Changed.
ESTRAGON: Very likely. They all change. Only we can't.
VLADIMIR: Likely! It's certain. Didn't you see them?
ESTRAGON: I suppose I did. But I don't know them.
VLADIMIR: Yes you do know them.
ESTRAGON: No I don't know them.
VLADIMIR: We know them, I tell you. You forget everything. (*Pause. To himself.*) Unless they're not the same . .
ESTRAGON: Why didn't they recognize us then?
VLADIMIR: That means nothing. I too pretended not to recognize them. And then nobody ever recognizes us.
ESTRAGON: Forget it. What we need—ow! (*Vladimir does not react.*) Ow!
VLADIMIR: (*to himself*). Unless they're not the same . . .
ESTRAGON: Didi! It's the other foot!
He goes hobbling towards the mound.
VLADIMIR: Unless they're not the same . . .
BOY: (*off*). Mister!
Estragon halts. Both look towards the voice.
ESTRAGON: Off we go again.

32

VLADIMIR: Approach, my child.
Enter Boy, timidly. He halts.
BOY: Mister Albert . . . ?
VLADIMIR: Yes.
ESTRAGON: What do you want?
VLADIMIR: Approach!
The Boy does not move.
ESTRAGON: (*forcibly*). Approach when you're told, can't you?
The Boy advances timidly, halts.
VLADIMIR: What is it?
BOY: Mr. Godot . . .
VLADIMIR: Obviously . . . (*Pause.*) Approach.
ESTRAGON: (*violently*). Will you approach! (*The Boy advances timidly.*) What kept you so late?
VLADIMIR: You have a message from Mr. Godot?
BOY: Yes Sir.
VLADIMIR: Well, what is it?
ESTRAGON: What kept you so late?
The Boy looks at them in turn, not knowing to which he should reply.
VLADIMIR: (*to Estragon*). Let him alone.
ESTRAGON: (*violently*). You let me alone. (*Advancing, to the Boy.*) Do you know what time it is?
BOY: (*recoiling*). It's not my fault, Sir.
ESTRAGON: And whose is it? Mine?
BOY: I was afraid, Sir.
ESTRAGON: Afraid of what? Of us? (*Pause.*) Answer me!
VLADIMIR: I know what it is, he was afraid of the others.
ESTRAGON: How long have you been here?
BOY: A good while, Sir.

VLADIMIR: You were afraid of the whip?

BOY: Yes Sir.

VLADIMIR: The roars?

BOY: Yes Sir.

VLADIMIR: The two big men.

BOY: Yes Sir.

VLADIMIR: Do you know them?

BOY: No Sir.

VLADIMIR: Are you a native of these parts? (*Silence.*) Do you belong to these parts?

BOY: Yes Sir.

ESTRAGON: That's all a pack of lies. (*Shaking the Boy by the arm.*) Tell us the truth!

BOY: (*trembling*). But it is the truth, Sir!

VLADIMIR: Will you let him alone! What's the matter with you? (*Estragon releases the Boy, moves away, covering his face with his hands. Vladimir and the Boy observe him. Estragon drops his hands. His face is convulsed.*) What's the matter with you?

ESTRAGON: I'm unhappy.

VLADIMIR: Not really! Since when?

ESTRAGON: I'd forgotten.

VLADIMIR: Extraordinary the tricks that memory plays! (*Estragon tries to speak, renounces, limps to his place, sits down and begins to take off his boots. To Boy.*) Well?

BOY: Mr. Godot—

VLADIMIR: I've seen you before, haven't I?

BOY: I don't know, Sir.

VLADIMIR: You don't know me?

BOY: No Sir.

VLADIMIR: It wasn't you came yesterday?

BOY: No Sir.

VLADIMIR: This is your first time?

BOY: Yes Sir.

Silence.

VLADIMIR: Words words. (*Pause.*) Speak.

BOY: (*in a rush*). Mr. Godot told me to tell you he won't come this evening but surely to-morrow.

Silence.

VLADIMIR: Is that all?

BOY: Yes Sir.

Silence.

VLADIMIR: You work for Mr. Godot?

BOY: Yes Sir.

VLADIMIR: What do you do?

BOY: I mind the goats, Sir.

VLADIMIR: Is he good to you?

BOY: Yes Sir.

VLADIMIR: He doesn't beat you?

BOY: No Sir, not me.

VLADIMIR: Whom does he beat?

BOY: He beats my brother, Sir.

VLADIMIR: Ah, you have a brother?

BOY: Yes Sir.

VLADIMIR: What does he do?

BOY: He minds the sheep, Sir.

VLADIMIR: And why doesn't he beat you?

BOY: I don't know, Sir.

VLADIMIR: He must be fond of you.

BOY: I don't know, Sir.

Silence.

VLADIMIR: Does he give you enough to eat? (*The Boy hesitates.*) Does he feed you well?

BOY: Fairly well, Sir.

VLADIMIR: You're not unhappy? (*The Boy hesitates.*) Do you hear me?

BOY: Yes Sir.

VLADIMIR: Well?

BOY: I don't know, Sir.

VLADIMIR: You don't know if you're unhappy or not?

BOY: No Sir.

VLADIMIR: You're as bad as myself. (*Silence.*) Where do you sleep?

BOY: In the loft, Sir.

VLADIMIR: With your brother?

BOY: Yes Sir.

VLADIMIR: In the hay?

BOY: Yes Sir.

Silence.

VLADIMIR: All right, you may go.

BOY: What am I to tell Mr. Godot, Sir?

VLADIMIR: Tell him . . . (*he hesitates*) . . . tell him you saw us. (*Pause.*) You did see us, didn't you?

BOY: Yes Sir.

He steps back, hesitates, turns and exit running. The light suddenly fails. In a moment it is night. The moon rises at back, mounts in the sky, stands still, shedding a pale light on the scene.

34

VLADIMIR: At last! (*Estragon gets up and goes towards Vladimir, a boot in each hand. He puts them down at edge of stage, straightens and contemplates the moon.*) What are you doing?

ESTRAGON: Pale for weariness.

VLADIMIR: Eh?

ESTRAGON: Of climbing heaven and gazing on the likes of us.

VLADIMIR: Your boots, what are you doing with your boots?

ESTRAGON: (*turning to look at the boots*). I'm leaving them there. (*Pause.*) Another will come, just as . . . as . . . as me, but with smaller feet, and they'll make him happy.

VLADIMIR: But you can't go barefoot!

ESTRAGON: Christ did.

VLADIMIR: Christ! What has Christ got to do with it? You're not going to compare yourself to Christ!

ESTRAGON: All my life I've compared myself to him.

VLADIMIR: But where he lived it was warm, it was dry!

ESTRAGON: Yes. And they crucified quick.
        Silence.

VLADIMIR: We've nothing more to do here.

ESTRAGON: Nor anywhere else.

VLADIMIR: Ah Gogo, don't go on like that. To-morrow everything will be better.

ESTRAGON: How do you make that out?

VLADIMIR: Did you not hear what the child said?

ESTRAGON: No.

VLADIMIR: He said that Godot was sure to come to-morrow. (*Pause.*) What do you say to that?

ESTRAGON: Then all we have to do is to wait on here.

VLADIMIR: Are you mad? We must take cover. (*He takes Estragon by the arm.*) Come on.
He draws Estragon after him. Estragon yields, then resists. They halt.

ESTRAGON: (*looking at the tree*). Pity we haven't got a bit of rope.

VLADIMIR: Come on. It's cold.
He draws Estragon after him. As before.

ESTRAGON: Remind me to bring a bit of rope to-morrow.

VLADIMIR: Yes. Come on.
He draws him after him. As before.

ESTRAGON: How long have we been together all the time now?

VLADIMIR: I don't know. Fifty years maybe.

ESTRAGON: Do you remember the day I threw myself into the Rhone?

VLADIMIR: We were grape harvesting.

ESTRAGON: You fished me out.

VLADIMIR: That's all dead and buried.

ESTRAGON: My clothes dried in the sun.

VLADIMIR: There's no good harking back on that. Come on.
He draws him after him. As before.

ESTRAGON: Wait!

VLADIMIR: I'm cold!

ESTRAGON: Wait! (*He moves away from Vladimir.*) I sometimes wonder if we wouldn't have been better off alone, each one for himself. (*He crosses the stage and sits down on the mound.*) We weren't made for the same road.

VLADIMIR: *(without anger)*. It's not certain.

ESTRAGON: No, nothing is certain.

Vladimir slowly crosses the stage and sits down beside Estragon.

VLADIMIR: We can still part, if you think it would be better.

ESTRAGON: It's not worth while now.

Silence.

VLADIMIR: No, it's not worth while now.

Silence.

ESTRAGON: Well, shall we go?

VLADIMIR: Yes, let's go.

They do not move.

Curtain

ACT II

Next day. Same time.

Same place.

Estragon's boots front center, heels together, toes splayed. Lucky's hat at same place.
The tree has four or five leaves.
Enter Vladimir agitatedly. He halts and looks long at the tree, then suddenly begins to move feverishly about the stage. He halts before the boots, picks one up, examines it, sniffs it, manifests disgust, puts it back carefully. Comes and goes. Halts extreme right and gazes into distance off, shading his eyes with his hand. Comes and goes. Halts extreme left, as before. Comes and goes. Halts suddenly and begins to sing loudly.

VLADIMIR: A dog came in—
Having begun too high he stops, clears his throat, resumes:

> A dog came in the kitchen
> And stole a crust of bread.
> Then cook up with a ladle
> And beat him till he was dead.

> Then all the dogs came running
> And dug the dog a tomb—

He stops, broods, resumes:

> Then all the dogs came running
> And dug the dog a tomb
> And wrote upon the tombstone
> For the eyes of dogs to come:

> A dog came in the kitchen
> And stole a crust of bread.

37

Then cook up with a ladle
And beat him till he was dead.

Then all the dogs came running
And dug the dog a tomb—
He stops, broods, resumes:
Then all the dogs came running
And dug the dog a tomb—
He stops, broods. Softly.
And dug the dog a tomb . . .
He remains a moment silent and motionless, then begins to move feverishly about the stage. He halts before the tree, comes and goes, before the boots, comes and goes, halts extreme right, gazes into distance, extreme left, gazes into distance. Enter Estragon right, barefoot, head bowed. He slowly crosses the stage. Vladimir turns and sees him.

VLADIMIR: You again! (*Estragon halts but does not raise his head. Vladimir goes towards him.*) Come here till I embrace you.

ESTRAGON: Don't touch me!
Vladimir holds back, pained.

VLADIMIR: Do you want me to go away? (*Pause.*) Gogo! (*Pause. Vladimir observes him attentively.*) Did they beat you? (*Pause.*) Gogo! (*Estragon remains silent, head bowed.*) Where did you spend the night?

ESTRAGON: Don't touch me! Don't question me! Don't speak to me! Stay with me!

VLADIMIR: Did I ever leave you?

ESTRAGON: You let me go.

VLADIMIR: Look at me. (*Estragon does not raise his head. Violently.*) Will you look at me!
Estragon raises his head. They look long at each other, then suddenly embrace, clapping each other on the back. End of the embrace. Estragon, no longer supported, almost falls.

ESTRAGON: What a day!

VLADIMIR: Who beat you? Tell me.

ESTRAGON: Another day done with.

VLADIMIR: Not yet.

ESTRAGON: For me it's over and done with, no matter what happens. (*Silence.*) I heard you singing.

VLADIMIR: That's right, I remember.

ESTRAGON: That finished me. I said to myself, He's all alone, he thinks I'm gone for ever, and he sings.

VLADIMIR: One is not master of one's moods. All day I've felt in great form. (*Pause.*) I didn't get up in the night, not once!

ESTRAGON: (*sadly*). You see, you piss better when I'm not there.

VLADIMIR: I missed you . . . and at the same time I was happy. Isn't that a queer thing?

ESTRAGON: (*shocked*). Happy?

VLADIMIR: Perhaps it's not quite the right word.

ESTRAGON: And now?

VLADIMIR: Now? . . . (*Joyous.*) There you are again . . . (*Indifferent.*) There we are again . . . (*Gloomy.*) There I am again.

ESTRAGON: You see, you feel worse when I'm with you. I feel better alone too.

VLADIMIR: (*vexed*). Then why do you always come crawling back?

ESTRAGON: I don't know

VLADIMIR: No, but I do. It's because you don't know how to defend yourself. I wouldn't have let them beat you.

ESTRAGON: You couldn't have stopped them.

VLADIMIR: Why not?

ESTRAGON: There was ten of them.

VLADIMIR: No, I mean before they beat you. I would have stopped you from doing whatever it was you were doing.

ESTRAGON: I wasn't doing anything.

VLADIMIR: Then why did they beat you?

ESTRAGON: I don't know.

VLADIMIR: Ah no, Gogo, the truth is there are things escape you that don't escape me, you must feel it yourself.

ESTRAGON: I tell you I wasn't doing anything.

VLADIMIR: Perhaps you weren't. But it's the way of doing it that counts, the way of doing it, if you want to go on living.

ESTRAGON: I wasn't doing anything.

VLADIMIR: You must be happy too, deep down, if you only knew it.

ESTRAGON: Happy about what?

VLADIMIR: To be back with me again.

ESTRAGON: Would you say so?

VLADIMIR: Say you are, even if it's not true.

ESTRAGON: What am I to say?

VLADIMIR: Say, I am happy.

ESTRAGON: I am happy.

VLADIMIR: So am I.

ESTRAGON: So am I.

VLADIMIR: We are happy.

ESTRAGON: We are happy. (*Silence.*) What do we do now, now that we are happy?

VLADIMIR: Wait for Godot. (*Estragon groans. Silence.*) Things have changed here since yesterday.

ESTRAGON: And if he doesn't come.

VLADIMIR: (*after a moment of bewilderment*). We'll see when the time comes. (*Pause.*) I was saying that things have changed here since yesterday.

ESTRAGON: Everything oozes.

VLADIMIR: Look at the tree.

ESTRAGON: It's never the same pus from one second to the next.

VLADIMIR: The tree, look at the tree.
Estragon looks at the tree.

ESTRAGON: Was it not there yesterday?

VLADIMIR: Yes of course it was there. Do you not remember? We nearly hanged ourselves from it. But you wouldn't. Do you not remember?

ESTRAGON: You dreamt it.

VLADIMIR: Is it possible you've forgotten already?

ESTRAGON: That's the way I am. Either I forget immediately or I never forget.

VLADIMIR:	And Pozzo and Lucky, have you forgotten them too?
ESTRAGON:	Pozzo and Lucky?
VLADIMIR:	He's forgotten everything!
ESTRAGON:	I remember a lunatic who kicked the shins off me. Then he played the fool.
VLADIMIR:	That was Lucky.
ESTRAGON:	I remember that. But when was it?
VLADIMIR:	And his keeper, do you not remember him?
ESTRAGON:	He gave me a bone.
VLADIMIR:	That was Pozzo.
ESTRAGON:	And all that was yesterday, you say?
VLADIMIR:	Yes of course it was yesterday.
ESTRAGON:	And here where we are now?
VLADIMIR:	Where else do you think? Do you not recognize the place?
ESTRAGON:	(*suddenly furious*). Recognize! What is there to recognize? All my lousy life I've crawled about in the mud! And you talk to me about scenery! (*Looking wildly about him.*) Look at this muckheap! I've never stirred from it!
VLADIMIR:	Calm yourself, calm yourself.
ESTRAGON:	You and your landscapes! Tell me about the worms!
VLADIMIR:	All the same, you can't tell me that this (*gesture*) bears any resemblance to . . . (*he hesitates*) . . . to the Macon country for example. You can't deny there's a big difference.
ESTRAGON:	The Macon country! Who's talking to you about the Macon country?

VLADIMIR: But you were there yourself, in the Macon country.

ESTRAGON: No I was never in the Macon country! I've puked my puke of a life away here, I tell you! Here! In the Cackon country!

VLADIMIR: But we were there together, I could swear to it! Picking grapes for a man called . . . (*he snaps his fingers*) . . . can't think of the name of the man, at a place called . . . (*snaps his fingers*) . . . can't think of the name of the place, do you not remember?

ESTRAGON: (*a little calmer*). It's possible. I didn't notice anything.

VLADIMIR: But down there everything is red!

ESTRAGON: (*exasperated*). I didn't notice anything, I tell you! *Silence. Vladimir sighs deeply.*

VLADIMIR: You're a hard man to get on with, Gogo.

ESTRAGON: It'd be better if we parted.

VLADIMIR: You always say that and you always come crawling back.

ESTRAGON: The best thing would be to kill me, like the other.

VLADIMIR: What other? (*Pause.*) What other?

ESTRAGON: Like billions of others.

VLADIMIR: (*sententious*). To every man his little cross. (*He sighs.*) Till he dies. (*Afterthought.*) And is forgotten.

ESTRAGON: In the meantime let us try and converse calmly, since we are incapable of keeping silent.

VLADIMIR: You're right, we're inexhaustible.

ESTRAGON: It's so we won't think.

VLADIMIR: We have that excuse.

ESTRAGON: It's so we won't hear.

VLADIMIR: We have our reasons.

ESTRAGON: All the dead voices.

VLADIMIR: They make a noise like wings.

ESTRAGON: Like leaves.

VLADIMIR: Like sand.

ESTRAGON: Like leaves.

Silence.

VLADIMIR: They all speak at once.

ESTRAGON: Each one to itself.

Silence.

VLADIMIR: Rather they whisper.

ESTRAGON: They rustle.

VLADIMIR: They murmur.

ESTRAGON: They rustle.

Silence.

VLADIMIR: What do they say?

ESTRAGON: They talk about their lives.

VLADIMIR: To have lived is not enough for them.

ESTRAGON: They have to talk about it.

VLADIMIR: To be dead is not enough for them.

ESTRAGON: It is not sufficient.

Silence.

VLADIMIR: They make a noise like feathers.

ESTRAGON: Like leaves.

VLADIMIR: Like ashes.

ESTRAGON: Like leaves.

Long silence.

VLADIMIR: Say something!

ESTRAGON: I'm trying.
          Long silence.
VLADIMIR: (*in anguish*). Say anything at all!
ESTRAGON: What do we do now?
VLADIMIR: Wait for Godot.
ESTRAGON: Ah!
          Silence.
VLADIMIR: This is awful!
ESTRAGON: Sing something.
VLADIMIR: No no! (*He reflects.*) We could start all over again
          perhaps.
ESTRAGON: That should be easy.
VLADIMIR: It's the start that's difficult.
ESTRAGON: You can start from anything.
VLADIMIR: Yes, but you have to decide.
ESTRAGON: True.
          Silence.
VLADIMIR: Help me!
ESTRAGON: I'm trying.
          Silence.
VLADIMIR: When you seek you hear.
ESTRAGON: You do.
VLADIMIR: That prevents you from finding.
ESTRAGON: It does.
VLADIMIR: That prevents you from thinking.
ESTRAGON: You think all the same.
VLADIMIR: No no, impossible.
ESTRAGON: That's the idea, let's contradict each other.
VLADIMIR: Impossible.
ESTRAGON: You think so?

VLADIMIR: We're in no danger of ever thinking **any more.**

ESTRAGON: Then what are we complaining about?

VLADIMIR: Thinking is not the worst.

ESTRAGON: Perhaps not. But at least there's that.

VLADIMIR: That what?

ESTRAGON: That's the idea, let's ask each other questions.

VLADIMIR: What do you mean, at least there's that?

ESTRAGON: That much less misery.

VLADIMIR: True.

ESTRAGON: Well? If we gave thanks for our mercies?

VLADIMIR: What is terrible is to *have* thought.

ESTRAGON: But did that ever happen to us?

VLADIMIR: Where are all these corpses from?

ESTRAGON: These skeletons.

VLADIMIR: Tell me that.

ESTRAGON: True.

VLADIMIR: We must have thought a little.

ESTRAGON: At the very beginning.

VLADIMIR: A charnel-house! A charnel-house!

ESTRAGON: You don't have to look.

VLADIMIR: You can't help looking.

ESTRAGON: True.

VLADIMIR: Try as one may.

ESTRAGON: I beg your pardon?

VLADIMIR: Try as one may.

ESTRAGON: We should turn resolutely towards Nature.

VLADIMIR: We've tried that.

ESTRAGON: True.

VLADIMIR: Oh it's not the worst, I know.

ESTRAGON: What?

VLADIMIR: To have thought.

ESTRAGON: Obviously.

VLADIMIR: But we could have done without it.

ESTRAGON: Que voulez-vous?

VLADIMIR: I beg your pardon?

ESTRAGON: Que voulez-vous.

VLADIMIR: Ah! que voulez-vous. Exactly.
Silence.

ESTRAGON: That wasn't such a bad little canter.

VLADIMIR: Yes, but now we'll have to find something else.

ESTRAGON: Let me see.
He takes off his hat, concentrates.

VLADIMIR: Let me see. (*He takes off his hat, concentrates. Long silence.*) Ah!
They put on their hats, relax.

ESTRAGON: Well?

VLADIMIR: What was I saying, we could go on from there.

ESTRAGON: What were you saying when?

VLADIMIR: At the very beginning.

ESTRAGON: The very beginning of WHAT?

VLADIMIR: This evening . . . I was saying . . . I was saying . . .

ESTRAGON: I'm not a historian.

VLADIMIR: Wait . . . we embraced . . . we were happy . . . happy . . . what do we do now that we're happy . . . go on waiting . . . waiting . . . let me think . . . it's coming . . . go on waiting . . . now that we're happy . . . let me see . . . ah! The tree!

ESTRAGON: The tree?

VLADIMIR: Do you not remember?

ESTRAGON: I'm tired.

VLADIMIR: Look at it.

They look at the tree.

ESTRAGON: I see nothing.

VLADIMIR: But yesterday evening it was all black and bare. And now it's covered with leaves.

ESTRAGON: Leaves?

VLADIMIR: In a single night.

ESTRAGON: It must be the Spring.

VLADIMIR: But in a single night!

ESTRAGON: I tell you we weren't here yesterday. Another of your nightmares.

VLADIMIR: And where were we yesterday evening according to you?

ESTRAGON: How would I know? In another compartment. There's no lack of void.

VLADIMIR: (*sure of himself*). Good. We weren't here yesterday evening. Now what did we do yesterday evening?

ESTRAGON: Do?

VLADIMIR: Try and remember.

ESTRAGON: Do . . . I suppose we blathered.

VLADIMIR: (*controlling himself*). About what?

ESTRAGON: Oh . . . this and that I suppose, nothing in particular. (*With assurance.*) Yes, now I remember, yesterday evening we spent blathering about nothing in particular. That's been going on now for half a century.

VLADIMIR: You don't remember any fact, any circumstance?

ESTRAGON: (*weary*). Don't torment me, Didi.

VLADIMIR: The sun. The moon. Do you not remember?

ESTRAGON: They must have been there, as usual.

VLADIMIR: You didn't notice anything out of the ordinary?

ESTRAGON: Alas!

VLADIMIR: And Pozzo? And Lucky?

ESTRAGON: Pozzo?

VLADIMIR: The bones.

ESTRAGON: They were like fishbones.

VLADIMIR: It was Pozzo gave them to you.

ESTRAGON: I don't know.

VLADIMIR: And the kick.

ESTRAGON: That's right, someone gave me a kick.

VLADIMIR: It was Lucky gave it to you.

ESTRAGON: And all that was yesterday?

VLADIMIR: Show your leg.

ESTRAGON: Which?

VLADIMIR: Both. Pull up your trousers. (*Estragon gives a leg to Vladimir, staggers. Vladimir takes the leg. They stagger.*) Pull up your trousers.

ESTRAGON: I can't.

Vladimir pulls up the trousers, looks at the leg, lets it go. Estragon almost falls.

VLADIMIR: The other. (*Estragon gives the same leg.*) The other, pig! (*Estragon gives the other leg. Triumphantly.*) There's the wound! Beginning to fester!

ESTRAGON: And what about it?

VLADIMIR: (*letting go the leg*). Where are your boots?

ESTRAGON: I must have thrown them away.

43

VLADIMIR: When?

ESTRAGON: I don't know.

VLADIMIR: Why?

ESTRAGON: (*exasperated*). I don't know why I don't know!

VLADIMIR: No, I mean why did you throw them away?

ESTRAGON: (*exasperated*). Because they were hurting me!

VLADIMIR: (*triumphantly, pointing to the boots*). There they are! (*Estragon looks at the boots.*) At the very spot where you left them yesterday!
Estragon goes towards the boots, inspects them closely.

ESTRAGON: They're not mine.

VLADIMIR: (*stupefied*). Not yours!

ESTRAGON: Mine were black. These are brown.

VLADIMIR: You're sure yours were black?

ESTRAGON: Well they were a kind of gray.

VLADIMIR: And these are brown. Show.

ESTRAGON: (*picking up a boot*). Well they're a kind of green.

VLADIMIR: Show. (*Estragon hands him the boot. Vladimir inspects it, throws it down angrily.*) Well of all the—

ESTRAGON: You see, all that's a lot of bloody—

VLADIMIR: Ah! I see what it is. Yes, I see what's happened.

ESTRAGON: All that's a lot of bloody—

VLADIMIR: It's elementary. Someone came and took yours and left you his.

ESTRAGON: Why?

VLADIMIR: His were too tight for him, so he took yours.

ESTRAGON: But mine were too tight.

VLADIMIR: For you. Not for him.

ESTRAGON: (*having tried in vain to work it out*). I'm tired! (*Pause.*) Let's go.

VLADIMIR: We can't.

ESTRAGON: Why not?

VLADIMIR: We're waiting for Godot.

ESTRAGON: Ah! (*Pause. Despairing.*) What'll we do, what'll we do!

VLADIMIR: There's nothing we can do.

ESTRAGON: But I can't go on like this!

VLADIMIR: Would you like a radish?

ESTRAGON: Is that all there is?

VLADIMIR: There are radishes and turnips.

ESTRAGON: Are there no carrots?

VLADIMIR: No. Anyway you overdo it with your carrots.

ESTRAGON: Then give me a radish. (*Vladimir fumbles in his pockets, finds nothing but turnips, finally brings out a radish and hands it to Estragon who examines it, sniffs it.*) It's black!

VLADIMIR: It's a radish.

ESTRAGON: I only like the pink ones, you know that!

VLADIMIR: Then you don't want it?

ESTRAGON: I only like the pink ones!

VLADIMIR: Then give it back to me.
Estragon gives it back.

ESTRAGON: I'll go and get a carrot.
He does not move.

VLADIMIR: This is becoming really insignificant.

ESTRAGON: Not enough.
Silence.

VLADIMIR: What about trying them.

44

ESTRAGON: I've tried everything.

VLADIMIR: No, I mean the boots.

ESTRAGON: Would that be a good thing?

VLADIMIR: It'd pass the time. (*Estragon hesitates.*) I assure you, it'd be an occupation.

ESTRAGON: A relaxation.

VLADIMIR: A recreation.

ESTRAGON: A relaxation.

VLADIMIR: Try.

ESTRAGON: You'll help me?

VLADIMIR: I will of course.

ESTRAGON: We don't manage too badly, eh Didi, between the two of us?

VLADIMIR: Yes yes. Come on, we'll try the left first.

ESTRAGON: We always find something, eh Didi, to give us the impression we exist?

VLADIMIR: (*impatiently*). Yes yes, we're magicians. But let us persevere in what we have resolved, before we forget. (*He picks up a boot.*) Come on, give me your foot. (*Estragon raises his foot.*) The other, hog! (*Estragon raises the other foot.*) Higher! (*Wreathed together they stagger about the stage. Vladimir succeeds finally in getting on the boot.*) Try and walk. (*Estragon walks.*) Well?

ESTRAGON: It fits.

VLADIMIR: (*taking string from his pocket*). We'll try and lace it.

ESTRAGON: (*vehemently*). No no, no laces, no laces!

VLADIMIR: You'll be sorry. Let's try the other. (*As before.*) Well?

ESTRAGON: (*grudgingly*). It fits too.

VLADIMIR: They don't hurt you?

ESTRAGON: Not yet.

VLADIMIR: Then you can keep them.

ESTRAGON: They're too big.

VLADIMIR: Perhaps you'll have socks some day.

ESTRAGON: True.

VLADIMIR: Then you'll keep them?

ESTRAGON: That's enough about these boots.

VLADIMIR: Yes, but—

ESTRAGON: (*violently*). Enough! (*Silence.*) I suppose I might as well sit down.

He looks for a place to sit down, then goes and sits down on the mound.

VLADIMIR: That's where you were sitting yesterday evening.

ESTRAGON: If I could only sleep.

VLADIMIR: Yesterday you slept.

ESTRAGON: I'll try.

He resumes his foetal posture, his head between his knees.

VLADIMIR: Wait. (*He goes over and sits down beside Estragon and begins to sing in a loud voice.*)

> Bye bye bye bye
> Bye bye—

ESTRAGON: (*looking up angrily*). Not so loud!

VLADIMIR: (*softly*).

> Bye bye bye bye
> Bye bye bye bye
> Bye bye bye bye
> Bye bye . . .

Estragon sleeps. Vladimir gets up softly, takes off his coat and lays it across Estragon's shoulders, then starts walking up and down, swinging his arms to keep himself warm. Estragon wakes with a start, jumps up, casts about wildly. Vladimir runs to him, puts his arms round him.) There . . . there . . . Didi is there . . . don't be afraid . . .

ESTRAGON: Ah!

VLADIMIR: There . . . there . . . it's all over.

ESTRAGON: I was falling—

VLADIMIR: It's all over, it's all over.

ESTRAGON: I was on top of a—

VLADIMIR: Don't tell me! Come, we'll walk it off.
He takes Estragon by the arm and walks him up and down until Estragon refuses to go any further.

ESTRAGON: That's enough. I'm tired.

VLADIMIR: You'd rather be stuck there doing nothing?

ESTRAGON: Yes.

VLADIMIR: Please yourself.
He releases Estragon, picks up his coat and puts it on.

ESTRAGON: Let's go.

VLADIMIR: We can't.

ESTRAGON: Why not?

VLADIMIR: We're waiting for Godot.

ESTRAGON: Ah! *(Vladimir walks up and down.)* Can you not stay still?

VLADIMIR: I'm cold.

ESTRAGON: We came too soon.

VLADIMIR:	It's always at nightfall.
ESTRAGON:	But night doesn't fall.
VLADIMIR:	It'll fall all of a sudden, like yesterday.
ESTRAGON:	Then it'll be night.
VLADIMIR:	And we can go.
ESTRAGON:	Then it'll be day again. (*Pause. Despairing.*) What'll we do, what'll we do!
VLADIMIR:	(*halting, violently*). Will you stop whining! I've had about my bellyful of your lamentations!
ESTRAGON:	I'm going.
VLADIMIR:	(*seeing Lucky's hat*). Well!
ESTRAGON:	Farewell.
VLADIMIR:	Lucky's hat. (*He goes towards it.*) I've been here an hour and never saw it. (*Very pleased.*) Fine!
ESTRAGON:	You'll never see me again.
VLADIMIR:	I knew it was the right place. Now our troubles are over. (*He picks up the hat, contemplates it, straightens it.*) Must have been a very fine hat. (*He puts it on in place of his own which he hands to Estragon.*) Here.
ESTRAGON:	What?
VLADIMIR:	Hold that.

Estragon takes Vladimir's hat. Vladimir adjusts Lucky's hat on his head. Estragon puts on Vladimir's hat in place of his own which he hands to Vladimir. Vladimir takes Estragon's hat. Estragon adjusts Vladimir's hat on his head. Vladimir puts on Estragon's hat in place of Lucky's which he hands to Estragon. Estragon takes Lucky's hat. Vladimir adjusts Estragon's

hat on his head. Estragon puts on Lucky's hat in
place of Vladimir's which he hands to Vladimir.
Vladimir takes his hat. Estragon adjusts Lucky's
hat on his head. Vladimir puts on his hat in place
of Estragon's which he hands to Estragon.
Estragon takes his hat. Vladimir adjusts his hat
on his head. Estragon puts on his hat in place of
Lucky's which he hands to Vladimir. Vladimir
takes Lucky's hat. Estragon adjusts his hat on his
head. Vladimir puts on Lucky's hat in place of his
own which he hands to Estragon. Estragon takes
Vladimir's hat. Vladimir adjusts Lucky's hat on
his head. Estragon hands Vladimir's hat back to
Vladimir who takes it and hands it back to
Estragon who takes it and hands it back to
Vladimir who takes it and throws it down.
How does it fit me?

ESTRAGON: How would I know?

VLADIMIR: No, but how do I look in it?
He turns his head coquettishly to and fro, minces
like a mannequin.

ESTRAGON: Hideous.

VLADIMIR: Yes, but not more so than usual?

ESTRAGON: Neither more nor less.

VLADIMIR: Then I can keep it. Mine irked me. (*Pause.*) How
shall I say? (*Pause.*) It itched me.
He takes off Lucky's hat, peers into it, shakes it,
knocks on the crown, puts it on again.

ESTRAGON: I'm going.
Silence.

VLADIMIR:	Will you not play?
ESTRAGON:	Play at what?
VLADIMIR:	We could play at Pozzo and Lucky.
ESTRAGON:	Never heard of it.
VLADIMIR:	I'll do Lucky, you do Pozzo. (*He imitates Lucky sagging under the weight of his baggage. Estragon looks at him with stupefaction.*) Go on.
ESTRAGON:	What am I to do?
VLADIMIR:	Curse me!
ESTRAGON:	(*after reflection*). Naughty!
VLADIMIR:	Stronger!
ESTRAGON:	Gonococcus! Spirochete!
	Vladimir sways back and forth, doubled in two.
VLADIMIR:	Tell me to think.
ESTRAGON:	What?
VLADIMIR:	Say, Think, pig!
ESTRAGON:	Think, pig!
	Silence.
VLADIMIR:	I can't!
ESTRAGON:	That's enough of that.
VLADIMIR:	Tell me to dance.
ESTRAGON:	I'm going.
VLADIMIR:	Dance, hog! (*He writhes. Exit Estragon left, precipitately.*) I can't! (*He looks up, misses Estragon.*) Gogo! (*He moves wildly about the stage. Enter Estragon left, panting. He hastens towards Vladimir, falls into his arms.*) There you are again at last!
ESTRAGON:	I'm accursed!

VLADIMIR: Where were you? I thought you were gone for ever.

ESTRAGON: They're coming!

VLADIMIR: Who?

ESTRAGON: I don't know.

VLADIMIR: How many?

ESTRAGON: I don't know.

VLADIMIR: (*triumphantly*). It's Godot! At last! Gogo! It's Godot! We're saved! Let's go and meet him! (*He drags Estragon towards the wings. Estragon resists, pulls himself free, exit right.*) Gogo! Come back! (*Vladimir runs to extreme left, scans the horizon. Enter Estragon right, he hastens towards Vladimir, falls into his arms.*) There you are again again!

ESTRAGON: I'm in hell!

VLADIMIR: Where were you?

ESTRAGON: They're coming there too!

VLADIMIR: We're surrounded! (*Estragon makes a rush towards back.*) Imbecile! There's no way out there. (*He takes Estragon by the arm and drags him towards front. Gesture towards front.*) There! Not a soul in sight! Off you go! Quick! (*He pushes Estragon towards auditorium. Estragon recoils in horror.*) You won't? (*He contemplates auditorium.*) Well I can understand that. Wait till I see. (*He reflects.*) Your only hope left is to disappear.

ESTRAGON: Where?

VLADIMIR: Behind the tree. (*Estragon hesitates.*) Quick! Behind the tree. (*Estragon goes and crouches behind the tree, realizes he is not hidden, comes out from behind the tree.)* Decidedly this tree will not have been the slightest use to us.

ESTRAGON: *(calmer).* I lost my head. Forgive me. It won't happen again. Tell me what to do.

VLADIMIR: There's nothing to do.

ESTRAGON: You go and stand there. *(He draws Vladimir to extreme right and places him with his back to the stage.)* There, don't move, and watch out. *(Vladimir scans horizon, screening his eyes with his hand. Estragon runs and takes up same position extreme left. They turn their heads and look at each other.)* Back to back like in the good old days. *(They continue to look at each other for a moment, then resume their watch. Long silence.)* Do you see anything coming?

VLADIMIR: *(turning his head).* What?

ESTRAGON: *(louder).* Do you see anything coming?

VLADIMIR: No.

ESTRAGON: Nor I.
They resume their watch. Silence.

VLADIMIR: You must have had a vision.

ESTRAGON: *(turning his head).* What?

VLADIMIR: *(louder).* You must have had a vision.

ESTRAGON: No need to shout!
They resume their watch. Silence.

VLADIMIR:
ESTRAGON: *(turning simultaneously).* Do you—

VLADIMIR: Oh pardon!

ESTRAGON: Carry on.

VLADIMIR: No no, after you.
ESTRAGON: No no, you first.
VLADIMIR: I interrupted you.
ESTRAGON: On the contrary.

They glare at each other angrily.

VLADIMIR: Ceremonious ape!
ESTRAGON: Punctilious pig!
VLADIMIR: Finish your phrase, I tell you!
ESTRAGON: Finish your own!

Silence. They draw closer, halt.

VLADIMIR: Moron!
ESTRAGON: That's the idea, let's abuse each other.

They turn, move apart, turn again and face each other.

VLADIMIR: Moron!
ESTRAGON: Vermin!
VLADIMIR: Abortion!
ESTRAGON: Morpion!
VLADIMIR: Sewer-rat!
ESTRAGON: Curate!
VLADIMIR: Cretin!
ESTRAGON: *(with finality)*. Crritic!
VLADIMIR: Oh!

He wilts, vanquished, and turns away.

ESTRAGON: Now let's make it up.
VLADIMIR: Gogo!
ESTRAGON: Didi!
VLADIMIR: Your hand!
ESTRAGON: Take it!
VLADIMIR: Come to my arms!

ESTRAGON: Your arms?

VLADIMIR: My breast!

ESTRAGON: Off we go!

They embrace. They separate. Silence.

VLADIMIR: How time flies when one has fun!

Silence.

ESTRAGON: What do we do now?

VLADIMIR: While waiting.

ESTRAGON: While waiting.

Silence.

VLADIMIR: We could do our exercises.

ESTRAGON: Our movements.

VLADIMIR: Our elevations.

ESTRAGON: Our relaxations.

VLADIMIR: Our elongations.

ESTRAGON: Our relaxations.

VLADIMIR: To warm us up.

ESTRAGON: To calm us down.

VLADIMIR: Off we go.

Vladimir hops from one foot to the other Estragon imitates him.

ESTRAGON: (*stopping*). That's enough. I'm tired.

VLADIMIR: (*stopping*). We're not in form. What about a little deep breathing?

ESTRAGON: I'm tired breathing.

VLADIMIR: You're right. (*Pause.*) Let's just do the tree, for the balance.

ESTRAGON: The tree?

Vladimir does the tree, staggering about on one leg.

VLADIMIR: (*stopping*). Your turn.

Estragon does the tree, staggers.

ESTRAGON: Do you think God sees me?

VLADIMIR: You must close your eyes.

Estragon closes his eyes, staggers worse.

ESTRAGON: (*stopping, brandishing his fists, at the top of his voice*). God have pity on me!

VLADIMIR: (*vexed*). And me?

ESTRAGON: On me! On me! Pity! On me!

Enter Pozzo and Lucky. Pozzo is blind. Lucky burdened as before. Rope as before, but much shorter, so that Pozzo may follow more easily. Lucky wearing a different hat. At the sight of Vladimir and Estragon he stops short. Pozzo, continuing on his way, bumps into him.

VLADIMIR: Gogo!

POZZO: (*clutching on to Lucky who staggers*). What is it? Who is it?

Lucky falls, drops everything and brings down Pozzo with him. They lie helpless among the scattered baggage.

ESTRAGON: Is it Godot?

VLADIMIR: At last! (*He goes towards the heap.*) Reinforcements at last!

POZZO: Help!

ESTRAGON: Is it Godot?

VLADIMIR: We were beginning to weaken. Now we're sure to see the evening out.

POZZO: Help!

ESTRAGON: Do you hear him?

VLADIMIR: We are no longer alone, waiting for the night, waiting for Godot, waiting for . . . waiting. All evening we have struggled, unassisted. Now it's over. It's already to-morrow.

POZZO: Help!

VLADIMIR: Time flows again already. The sun will set, the moon rise, and we away . . . from here.

POZZO: Pity!

VLADIMIR: Poor Pozzo!

ESTRAGON: I knew it was him.

VLADIMIR: Who?

ESTRAGON: Godot.

VLADIMIR: But it's not Godot.

ESTRAGON: It's not Godot?

VLADIMIR: It's not Godot.

ESTRAGON: Then who is it?

VLADIMIR: It's Pozzo.

POZZO: Here! Here! Help me up!

VLADIMIR: He can't get up.

ESTRAGON: Let's go.

VLADIMIR: We can't.

ESTRAGON: Why not?

VLADIMIR: We're waiting for Godot.

ESTRAGON: Ah!

VLADIMIR: Perhaps he has another bone for you.

ESTRAGON: Bone?

VLADIMIR: Chicken. Do you not remember?

ESTRAGON: It was him?

VLADIMIR: Yes.

ESTRAGON: Ask him.

50

VLADIMIR: Perhaps we should help him first.

ESTRAGON: To do what?

VLADIMIR: To get up.

ESTRAGON: He can't get up?

VLADIMIR: He wants to get up.

ESTRAGON: Then let him get up.

VLADIMIR: He can't.

ESTRAGON: Why not?

VLADIMIR: I don't know.

Pozzo writhes, groans, beats the ground with his fists.

ESTRAGON: We should ask him for the bone first. Then if he refuses we'll leave him there.

VLADIMIR: You mean we have him at our mercy?

ESTRAGON: Yes.

VLADIMIR: And that we should subordinate our good offices to certain conditions?

ESTRAGON: What?

VLADIMIR: That seems intelligent all right. But there's one thing I'm afraid of.

POZZO: Help!

ESTRAGON: What?

VLADIMIR: That Lucky might get going all of a sudden. Then we'd be ballocksed.

ESTRAGON: Lucky?

VLADIMIR: The one that went for you yesterday.

ESTRAGON: I tell you there was ten of them.

VLADIMIR: No, before that, the one that kicked you.

ESTRAGON: Is he there?

VLADIMIR: As large as life. (*Gesture towards Lucky.*) For the moment he is inert. But he might run amuck any minute.

POZZO: Help!

ESTRAGON: And suppose we gave him a good beating the two of us?

VLADIMIR: You mean if we fell on him in his sleep?

ESTRAGON: Yes.

VLADIMIR: That seems a good idea all right. But could we do it? Is he really asleep? (*Pause.*) No, the best would be to take advantage of Pozzo's calling for help—

POZZO: Help!

VLADIMIR: To help him—

ESTRAGON: *We* help *him*?

VLADIMIR: In anticipation of some tangible return.

ESTRAGON: And suppose he—

VLADIMIR: Let us not waste our time in idle discourse! (*Pause. Vehemently.*) Let us do something, while we have the chance! It is not every day that we are needed. Not indeed that we personally are needed. Others would meet the case equally well, if not better. To all mankind they were addressed, those cries for help still ringing in our ears! But at this place, at this moment of time, all mankind is us, whether we like it or not. Let us make the most of it, before it is too late! Let us represent worthily for once the foul brood to which a cruel fate consigned us! What do you say? (*Estragon says nothing.*) It is true that when with folded arms we weigh the pros and cons we are no less a credit to our species. The tiger bounds to the help of his congeners without the least reflexion, or else he slinks away into the depths of the thickets. But that is not the question. What are we doing here, *that* is the question. And we are blessed in this, that we happen to know the answer. Yes, in this immense confusion one thing alone is clear. We are waiting for Godot to come—

ESTRAGON: Ah!

POZZO: Help!

VLADIMIR: Or for night to fall. (*Pause.*) We have kept our appointment and that's an end to that. We are not saints, but we have kept our appointment. How many people can boast as much?

ESTRAGON: Billions.

VLADIMIR: You think so?

ESTRAGON: I don't know.

VLADIMIR: You may be right.

POZZO: Help!

VLADIMIR: All I know is that the hours are long, under these conditions, and constrain us to beguile them with proceedings which—how shall I say—which may at first sight seem reasonable, until they become a habit. You may say it is to prevent our reason from foundering. No doubt. But has it not long been straying in the night without end of the abyssal depths? That's what I sometimes wonder. You follow my reasoning?

ESTRAGON: (*aphoristic for once*). We are all born mad. Some remain so.

POZZO: Help! I'll pay you!

ESTRAGON: How much?

POZZO: One hundred francs!

ESTRAGON: It's not enough.

VLADIMIR: I wouldn't go so far as that.

ESTRAGON: You think it's enough?

VLADIMIR: No, I mean so far as to assert that I was weak in the head when I came into the world. But that is not the question.

POZZO: Two hundred!

VLADIMIR: We wait. We are bored. (*He throws up his hand.*) No, don't protest, we are bored to death, there's no denying it. Good. A diversion comes along and what do we do? We let it go to waste. Come, let's get to work! (*He advances towards the heap, stops in his stride.*) In an instant all will vanish and we'll be alone once more, in the midst of nothingness!
He broods.

POZZO: Two hundred!

VLADIMIR: We're coming!
He tries to pull Pozzo to his feet, fails, tries again, stumbles, falls, tries to get up, fails.

ESTRAGON: What's the matter with you all?

VLADIMIR: Help!

ESTRAGON: I'm going.

VLADIMIR: Don't leave me! They'll kill me!

POZZO: Where am I?

VLADIMIR: Gogo!

POZZO: Help!

52

VLADIMIR: Help!

ESTRAGON: I'm going.

VLADIMIR: Help me up first, then we'll go together.

ESTRAGON: You promise?

VLADIMIR: I swear it!

ESTRAGON: And we'll never come back?

VLADIMIR: Never!

ESTRAGON: We'll go to the Pyrenees.

VLADIMIR: Wherever you like.

ESTRAGON: I've always wanted to wander in the Pyrenees.

VLADIMIR: You'll wander in them.

ESTRAGON: *(recoiling)*. Who farted?

VLADIMIR: Pozzo.

POZZO: Here! Here! Pity!

ESTRAGON: It's revolting!

VLADIMIR: Quick! Give me your hand!

ESTRAGON: I'm going. *(Pause. Louder.)* I'm going.

VLADIMIR: Well I suppose in the end I'll get up by myself. *(He tries, fails.)* In the fullness of time.

ESTRAGON: What's the matter with you?

VLADIMIR: Go to hell

ESTRAGON: Are you staying there?

VLADIMIR: For the time being.

ESTRAGON: Come on, get up, you'll catch a chill.

VLADIMIR: Don't worry about me.

ESTRAGON: Come on, Didi, don't be pig-headed!

He stretches out his hand which Vladimir makes haste to seize.

VLADIMIR: Pull!

Estragon pulls, stumbles, falls. Long silence.

POZZO: Help!

VLADIMIR: We've arrived.

POZZO: Who are you?

VLADIMIR: We are men.

           Silence.

ESTRAGON: Sweet mother earth!

VLADIMIR: Can you get up?

ESTRAGON: I don't know.

VLADIMIR: Try.

ESTRAGON: Not now, not now.

           Silence.

POZZO: What happened?

VLADIMIR: (*violently*). Will you stop it, you! Pest! He can
           think of nothing but himself!

ESTRAGON: What about a little snooze?

VLADIMIR: Did you hear him? He wants to know what
           happened!

ESTRAGON: Don't mind him. Sleep.

           Silence.

POZZO: Pity! Pity!

ESTRAGON: (*with a start*). What is it?

VLADIMIR: Were you asleep?

ESTRAGON: I must have been.

VLADIMIR: It's this bastard Pozzo at it again.

ESTRAGON: Make him stop it. Kick him in the crotch.

VLADIMIR: (*striking Pozzo*). Will you stop it! Crablouse!
           (*Pozzo extricates himself with cries of pain and
           crawls away. He stops, saws the air blindly,
           calling for help. Vladimir, propped on his elbow,*

53

observes his retreat.) He's off! (*Pozzo collapses.*)
He's down!

ESTRAGON: What do we do now?

VLADIMIR: Perhaps I could crawl to him.

ESTRAGON: Don't leave me!

VLADIMIR: Or I could call to him.

ESTRAGON: Yes, call to him.

VLADIMIR: Pozzo! (*Silence.*) Pozzo! (*Silence.*) No reply.

ESTRAGON: Together.

VLADIMIR:
ESTRAGON: Pozzo! Pozzo!

VLADIMIR: He moved.

ESTRAGON: Are you sure his name is Pozzo?

VLADIMIR: (*alarmed*). Mr. Pozzo! Come back! We won't hurt
you!
Silence.

ESTRAGON: We might try him with other names.

VLADIMIR: I'm afraid he's dying.

ESTRAGON: It'd be amusing.

VLADIMIR: What'd be amusing?

ESTRAGON: To try him with other names, one after the other.
It'd pass the time. And we'd be bound to hit on
the right one sooner or later.

VLADIMIR: I tell you his name is Pozzo.

ESTRAGON: We'll soon see. (*He reflects.*) Abel! Abel!

POZZO: Help!

ESTRAGON: Got it in one!

VLADIMIR: I begin to weary of this motif.

ESTRAGON: Perhaps the other is called Cain. Cain! Cain!

POZZO: Help!

ESTRAGON: He's all humanity. (*Silence.*) Look at the little cloud.

VLADIMIR: (*raising his eyes*). Where?

ESTRAGON: There. In the zenith.

VLADIMIR: Well? (*Pause.*) What is there so wonderful about it?

Silence.

ESTRAGON: Let's pass on now to something else, do you mind?

VLADIMIR: I was just going to suggest it.

ESTRAGON: But to what?

VLADIMIR: Ah!

Silence.

ESTRAGON: Suppose we got up to begin with?

VLADIMIR: No harm trying.

They get up.

ESTRAGON: Child's play.

VLADIMIR: Simple question of will-power.

ESTRAGON: And now?

POZZO: Help!

ESTRAGON: Let's go.

VLADIMIR: We can't.

ESTRAGON: Why not?

VLADIMIR: We're waiting for Godot.

ESTRAGON: Ah! (*Despairing.*) What'll we do, what'll we do!

POZZO: Help!

VLADIMIR: What about helping him?

ESTRAGON: What does he want?

VLADIMIR: He wants to get up.

ESTRAGON: Then why doesn't he?

54

VLADIMIR: He wants us to help him to get up.
ESTRAGON: Then why don't we? What are we waiting for?
They help Pozzo to his feet, let him go. He falls.
VLADIMIR: We must hold him. (*They get him up again. Pozzo sags between them, his arms round their necks.*) Feeling better?
POZZO: Who are you?
VLADIMIR: Do you not recognize us?
POZZO: I am blind.
Silence.
ESTRAGON: Perhaps he can see into the future.
VLADIMIR: Since when?
POZZO: I used to have wonderful sight—but are you friends?
ESTRAGON: (*laughing noisily*). He wants to know if we are friends!
VLADIMIR: No, he means friends of his.
ESTRAGON: Well?
VLADIMIR: We've proved we are, by helping him.
ESTRAGON: Exactly. Would we have helped him if we weren't his friends?
VLADIMIR: Possibly.
ESTRAGON: True.
VLADIMIR: Don't let's quibble about that now.
POZZO: You are not highwaymen?
ESTRAGON: Highwaymen! Do we look like highwaymen?
VLADIMIR: Damn it can't you see the man is blind!
ESTRAGON: Damn it so he is. (*Pause.*) So he says.
POZZO: Don't leave me!
VLADIMIR: No question of it.

ESTRAGON:	For the moment.
POZZO:	What time is it?
VLADIMIR:	(*inspecting the sky*). Seven o'clock . . . eight o'clock . . .
ESTRAGON:	That depends what time of year it is.
POZZO:	Is it evening?
	Silence. Vladimir and Estragon scrutinize the sunset.
ESTRAGON:	It's rising.
VLADIMIR:	Impossible.
ESTRAGON:	Perhaps it's the dawn.
VLADIMIR:	Don't be a fool. It's the west over there.
ESTRAGON:	How do you know?
POZZO:	(*anguished*). Is it evening?
VLADIMIR:	Anyway it hasn't moved.
ESTRAGON:	I tell you it's rising.
POZZO:	Why don't you answer me?
ESTRAGON:	Give us a chance.
VLADIMIR:	(*reassuring*). It's evening, Sir, it's evening, night is drawing nigh. My friend here would have me doubt it and I must confess he shook me for a moment. But it is not for nothing I have lived through this long day and I can assure you it is very near the end of its repertory. (*Pause.*) How do you feel now?
ESTRAGON:	How much longer are we to cart him around. (*They half release him, catch him again as he falls.*) We are not caryatids!
VLADIMIR:	You were saying your sight used to be good, if I heard you right.

POZZO: Wonderful! Wonderful, wonderful sight!
        Silence.
ESTRAGON: (*irritably*). Expand! Expand!
VLADIMIR: Let him alone. Can't you see he's thinking of the days when he was happy. (*Pause.*) *Memoria praeteritorum bonorum*—that must be unpleasant.
ESTRAGON: We wouldn't know.
VLADIMIR: And it came on you all of a sudden?
POZZO: Quite wonderful!
VLADIMIR: I'm asking you if it came on you all of a sudden.
POZZO: I woke up one fine day as blind as Fortune. (*Pause.*) Sometimes I wonder if I'm not still asleep.
VLADIMIR: And when was that?
POZZO: I don't know.
VLADIMIR: But no later than yesterday—
POZZO: (*violently*). Don't question me! The blind have no notion of time. The things of time are hidden from them too.
VLADIMIR: Well just fancy that! I could have sworn it was just the opposite.
ESTRAGON: I'm going.
POZZO: Where are we?
VLADIMIR: I couldn't tell you.
POZZO: It isn't by any chance the place known as the Board?
VLADIMIR: Never heard of it.
POZZO: What is it like?
VLADIMIR: (*looking round*). It's indescribable. It's like nothing. There's nothing. There's a tree.
POZZO: Then it's not the Board.

ESTRAGON: (*sagging*). Some diversion!

POZZO: Where is my menial?

VLADIMIR: He's about somewhere.

POZZO: Why doesn't he answer when I call?

VLADIMIR: I don't know. He seems to be sleeping. Perhaps he's dead.

POZZO: What happened exactly?

ESTRAGON: Exactly!

VLADIMIR: The two of you slipped. (*Pause.*) And fell.

POZZO: Go and see is he hurt.

VLADIMIR: We can't leave you.

POZZO: You needn't both go.

VLADIMIR: (*to Estragon*). You go.

ESTRAGON: After what he did to me? Never!

POZZO: Yes yes, let your friend go, he stinks so. (*Silence.*) What is he waiting for?

VLADIMIR: What you waiting for?

ESTRAGON. I'm waiting for Godot.

Silence.

VLADIMIR: What exactly should he do?

POZZO: Well to begin with he should pull on the rope, as hard as he likes so long as he doesn't strangle him. He usually responds to that. If not he should give him a taste of his boot, in the face and the privates as far as possible.

VLADIMIR: (*to Estragon*). You see, you've nothing to be afraid of. It's even an opportunity to revenge yourself.

ESTRAGON: And if he defends himself?

POZZO: No no, he never defends himself.

VLADIMIR: I'll come flying to the rescue.

56

ESTRAGON: Don't take your eyes off me.
He goes towards Lucky.

VLADIMIR: Make sure he's alive before you start. No point in exerting yourself if he's dead.

ESTRAGON: (*bending over Lucky*). He's breathing.

VLADIMIR: Then let him have it.
With sudden fury Estragon starts kicking Lucky, hurling abuse at him as he does so. But he hurts his foot and moves away, limping and groaning. Lucky stirs.

ESTRAGON: Oh the brute!
He sits down on the mound and tries to take off his boot. But he soon desists and disposes himself for sleep, his arms on his knees and his head on his arms.

POZZO: What's gone wrong now?

VLADIMIR: My friend has hurt himself.

POZZO: And Lucky?

VLADIMIR: So it is he?

POZZO: What?

VLADIMIR: It is Lucky?

POZZO: I don't understand.

VLADIMIR: And you are Pozzo?

POZZO: Certainly I am Pozzo.

VLADIMIR: The same as yesterday?

POZZO: Yesterday?

VLADIMIR: We met yesterday. (*Silence.*) Do you not remember?

POZZO: I don't remember having met anyone yesterday. But to-morrow I won't remember having met

anyone to-day. So don't count on me to enlighten
you.

VLADIMIR: But—

POZZO: Enough! Up pig!

VLADIMIR: You were bringing him to the fair to sell him. You
spoke to us. He danced. He thought. You had your
sight.

POZZO: As you please. Let me go! (*Vladimir moves away.*)
Up!
Lucky gets up, gathers up his burdens.

VLADIMIR: Where do you go from here.

POZZO: On. (*Lucky, laden down, takes his place before
Pozzo.*) Whip! (*Lucky puts everything down, looks
for whip, finds it, puts it into Pozzo's hand, takes
up everything again.*) Rope!
*Lucky puts everything down, puts end of rope
into Pozzo's hand, takes up everything again.*

VLADIMIR: What is there in the bag?

POZZO: Sand. (*He jerks the rope.*) On!

VLADIMIR: Don't go yet.

POZZO: I'm going.

VLADIMIR: What do you do when you fall far from help?

POZZO: We wait till we can get up. Then we go on. On!

VLADIMIR: Before you go tell him to sing.

POZZO: Who?

VLADIMIR: Lucky.

POZZO: To sing?

VLADIMIR: Yes. Or to think. Or to recite.

POZZO: But he is dumb.

VLADIMIR: Dumb!

POZZO: Dumb. He can't even groan.

VLADIMIR: Dumb! Since when?

POZZO: (*suddenly furious*). Have you not done tormenting me with your accursed time! It's abominable! When! When! One day, is that not enough for you, one day he went dumb, one day I went blind, one day we'll go deaf, one day we were born, one day we shall die, the same day, the same second, is that not enough for you? (*Calmer.*) They give birth astride of a grave, the light gleams an instant, then it's night once more. (*He jerks the rope.*) On!

Exeunt Pozzo and Lucky. Vladimir follows them to the edge of the stage, looks after them. The noise of falling, reinforced by mimic of Vladimir, announces that they are down again. Silence. Vladimir goes towards Estragon, contemplates him a moment, then shakes him awake.

ESTRAGON: (*wild gestures, incoherent words. Finally.*) Why will you never let me sleep?

VLADIMIR: I felt lonely.

ESTRAGON: I was dreaming I was happy.

VLADIMIR: That passed the time.

ESTRAGON: I was dreaming that—

VLADIMIR: (*violently*). Don't tell me! (*Silence.*) I wonder is he really blind.

ESTRAGON: Blind? Who?

VLADIMIR: Pozzo.

ESTRAGON: Blind?

VLADIMIR: He told us he was blind.

ESTRAGON: Well what about it?

VLADIMIR: It seemed to me he saw us.

ESTRAGON: You dreamt it. (*Pause.*) Let's go. We can't. **Ah!**
(*Pause.*) Are you sure it wasn't him?

VLADIMIR: Who?

ESTRAGON: Godot.

VLADIMIR: But who?

ESTRAGON: Pozzo.

VLADIMIR: Not at all! (*Less sure.*) Not at all! (*Still less sure.*)
Not at all!

ESTRAGON: I suppose I might as well get up. (*He gets up
painfully.*) Ow! Didi!

VLADIMIR: I don't know what to think any more.

ESTRAGON: My feet! (*He sits down again and tries to take off
his boots.*) Help me!

VLADIMIR: Was I sleeping, while the others suffered? Am I
sleeping now? To-morrow, when I wake, or think
I do, what shall I say of to-day? That with
Estragon my friend, at this place, until the fall of
night, I waited for Godot? That Pozzo passed,
with his carrier, and that he spoke to us? Probably.
But in all that what truth will there be?
(*Estragon, having struggled with his boots in vain,
is dozing off again. Vladimir looks at him.*) He'll
know nothing. He'll tell me about the blows he
received and I'll give him a carrot. (*Pause.*)
Astride of a grave and a difficult birth. Down in
the hole, lingeringly, the grave-digger puts on the
forceps. We have time to grow old. The air is full

of our cries. (*He listens.*) But habit is a great deadener. (*He looks again at Estragon.*) At me **too** someone is looking, of me too someone is saying, He is sleeping, he knows nothing, let him sleep on. (*Pause.*) I can't go on! (*Pause.*) What have I said?

He goes feverishly to and fro, halts finally at extreme left, broods. Enter Boy right. He halts. Silence.

BOY: Mister . . . (*Vladimir turns.*) Mister Albert . . .

VLADIMIR: Off we go again. (*Pause.*) Do you not recognize me?

BOY: No Sir.

VLADIMIR: It wasn't you came yesterday.

BOY: No Sir.

VLADIMIR: This is your first time.

BOY: Yes Sir.

Silence.

VLADIMIR: You have a message from Mr. Godot.

BOY: Yes Sir.

VLADIMIR: He won't come this evening.

BOY: No Sir.

VLADIMIR: But he'll come to-morrow.

BOY: Yes Sir.

VLADIMIR: Without fail.

BOY: Yes Sir.

Silence.

VLADIMIR: Did you meet anyone?

BOY: No Sir.

VLADIMIR: Two other . . . (*he hesitates*) . . . men?

BOY: I didn't see anyone, Sir.
Silence.

VLADIMIR: What does he do, Mr. Godot? (*Silence.*) Do you hear me?

BOY: Yes Sir.

VLADIMIR: Well?

BOY: He does nothing, Sir.
Silence.

VLADIMIR: How is your brother?

BOY: He's sick, Sir.

VLADIMIR: Perhaps it was he came yesterday.

BOY: I don't know, Sir.
Silence.

VLADIMIR: (*softly*). Has he a beard, Mr. Godot?

BOY: Yes Sir.

VLADIMIR: Fair or . . . (*he hesitates*) . . . or black?

BOY: I think it's white, Sir.
Silence.

VLADIMIR: Christ have mercy on us!
Silence.

BOY: What am I to tell Mr. Godot, Sir?

VLADIMIR: Tell him . . . (*he hesitates*) . . . tell him you saw me and that . . . (*he hesitates*) . . . that you saw me. (*Pause. Vladimir advances, the Boy recoils. Vladimir halts, the Boy halts. With sudden violence.*) You're sure you saw me, you won't come and tell me to-morrow that you never saw me! *Silence. Vladimir makes a sudden spring forward, the Boy avoids him and exit running. Silence. The*

*sun sets, the moon rises. As in Act 1. Vladimir
stands motionless and bowed. Estragon wakes,
takes off his boots, gets up with one in each hand
and goes and puts them down center front, then
goes towards Vladimir.*

ESTRAGON: What's wrong with you?

VLADIMIR: Nothing.

ESTRAGON: I'm going.

VLADIMIR: So am I.

ESTRAGON: Was I long asleep?

VLADIMIR: I don't know.
Silence.

ESTRAGON: Where shall we go?

VLADIMIR: Not far.

ESTRAGON: Oh yes, let's go far away from here.

VLADIMIR: We can't.

ESTRAGON: Why not?

VLADIMIR: We have to come back to-morrow.

ESTRAGON: What for?

VLADIMIR: To wait for Godot.

ESTRAGON: Ah! (*Silence.*) He didn't come?

VLADIMIR: No.

ESTRAGON: And now it's too late.

VLADIMIR: Yes, now it's night.

ESTRAGON: And if we dropped him? (*Pause.*) If we dropped
him?

VLADIMIR: He'd punish us. (*Silence. He looks at the tree.*)
Everything's dead but the tree.

ESTRAGON: (*looking at the tree*). What is it?

VLADIMIR: It's the tree.

ESTRAGON: Yes, but what kind?

VLADIMIR: I don't know. A willow.

Estragon draws Vladimir towards the tree. They stand motionless before it. Silence.

ESTRAGON: Why don't we hang ourselves?

VLADIMIR: With what?

ESTRAGON: You haven't got a bit of rope?

VLADIMIR: No.

ESTRAGON: Then we can't.

Silence.

VLADIMIR: Let's go.

ESTRAGON: Wait, there's my belt.

VLADIMIR: It's too short.

ESTRAGON: You could hang on to my legs.

VLADIMIR: And who'd hang on to mine?

ESTRAGON: True.

VLADIMIR: Show all the same. (*Estragon loosens the cord that holds up his trousers which, much too big for him, fall about his ankles. They look at the cord.*) It might do at a pinch. But is it strong enough?

ESTRAGON: We'll soon see. Here.

They each take an end of the cord and pull. It breaks. They almost fall.

VLADIMIR: Not worth a curse.

Silence.

ESTRAGON: You say we have to come back to-morrow?

VLADIMIR: Yes.

ESTRAGON: Then we can bring a good bit of rope.

VLADIMIR: Yes.

Silence.

60

ESTRAGON: Didi.

VLADIMIR: Yes.

ESTRAGON: I can't go on like this.

VLADIMIR: That's what you think.

ESTRAGON: If we parted? That might be better for us.

VLADIMIR: We'll hang ourselves to-morrow. (*Pause*.) Unless Godot comes.

ESTRAGON: And if he comes?

VLADIMIR: We'll be saved.

Vladimir takes off his hat (Lucky's), peers inside it, feels about inside it, shakes it, knocks on the crown, puts it on again.

ESTRAGON: Well? Shall we go?

VLADIMIR: Pull on your trousers.

ESTRAGON: What?

VLADIMIR: Pull on your trousers.

ESTRAGON: You want me to pull off my trousers?

VLADIMIR: Pull ON your trousers.

ESTRAGON: (*realizing his trousers are down*). True.

He pulls up his trousers.

VLADIMIR: Well? Shall we go?

ESTRAGON: Yes, let's go.

They do not move.

Curtain

WAITING FOR GODOT was first presented (as *En Attendant Godot*) at the Théâtre de Babylone, 38 Boulevard Raspail, Paris, France, during the season of 1952-3. The play was directed by Roger Blin, with décor by Sergio Gerstein. The cast was as follows:

ESTRAGON *Pierre Latour*

VLADIMIR *Lucien Raimbourg*

POZZO *Roger Blin*

LUCKY *Jean Martin*

A BOY *Serge Lecointe*

Samuel Beckett

Samuel Beckett was born in Dublin in 1906. He went to
Portora Royal School at Enniskillen, County Fermanagh
(Oscar Wilde's school), and to Trinity College, Dublin, from
which he graduated in 1927 with a B.A. in French and
Italian. From 1928 to 1930 he was in Paris at the École
Normale Supérieure as Lecteur d'Anglais, and his first book,
Whoroscope, a long poem, was printed there in 1930 by the
Hours Press (this press was directed by Nancy Cunard). The
following year he returned to Trinity College as lecturer in
French and took his M.A.; at that time his study of Proust was
published by Chatto and Windus. In 1932 he resigned his post
as lecturer and spent the next four years in London, France
and Germany, traveling about the Continent, and writing.
The book on Proust was followed by a collection of short
stories, *More Pricks than Kicks*, also published by Chatto and
Windus, and some poems, *Echo's Bones*, published by the
Europa Press, London. In 1937 he settled definitely in Paris
but was still writing in English; Routledge printed *Murphy*,
a novel, in 1938. During the war he lived in Paris until 1942
and translated *Murphy* into French. From 1942 to 1944 he was
in the Vaucluse (Unoccupied Zone) and there finished his last
work in English, *Watt*, a novel, published by Collection
Merlin in 1953. In 1945-46 he worked as storekeeper and
interpreter with the Irish Red Cross Hospital at St. Lô. When
he went back to Paris in 1947, the French translation of
Murphy was published by Editions Bordas, and since then
there have followed four more works in his adopted language,

all published by Les Editions de Minuit: the trilogy of novels, *Molloy* (1951), *Malone Meurt* (1952), *L'Innommable* (1953); and the play, *En Attendant Godot*. His trilogy has been translated into English and is published in America by Grove Press. The play, which ran over three hundred performances in Paris, has toured all over Europe, and has been widely performed in the United States. Since *En Attendant Godot*, Beckett has written two other stage plays, *Fin de Partie* and *Krapp's Last Tape*, as well as several radio plays.

Some of Beckett's short stories, as well as extracts from his novels, have been published in numerous French magazines, including *Les Temps Modernes, La Nouvelle N.R.F., Les Lettres Nouvelles, Fontaine,* and others, and articles on his work are frequent in France; since the war he has been published in English in *Transition* (Paris), *Envoy* (Dublin), *Irish Writing* (Cork), *Merlin* (Paris), *Evergreen Review* (New York), and *New World Writing* (New York).

OTHER GROVE PRESS DRAMA AND THEATER PAPERBACKS

B414	BRECHT, BERTOLT / The Mother / $2.95
B333	BRECHT, BERTOLT / The Threepenny Opera / $1.95
B193	BULGAKOV, MIKHAIL / Heart of a Dog / $2.95
B147	BULGAKOV, MIKHAIL / The Master and Margarita / $3.95
E773	CLURMAN, HAROLD, ed. / Nine Plays of the Modern Theater (Waiting for Godot by Samuel Beckett, The Visit by Friedrich Dürrenmatt, Tango by Slawomir Mrozek, The Caucasian Chalk Circle by Bertolt Brecht, The Balcony by Jean Genet, Rhinoceros by Eugene Ionesco, American Buffalo by David Mamet, The Birthday Party by Harold Pinter, and Rosencrantz and Guildenstern are Dead by Tom Stoppard) / $11.95
B459	COWARD, NOEL / Plays: One (Hay Fever, The Vortex, Fallen Angels, Easy Virtue) / $6.50
B460	COWARD, NOEL / Plays: Two (Private Lives, Bitter-Sweet, The Marquise, Post Mortem) / $6.50
B461	COWARD, NOEL / Plays: Three (Design for Living, Cavalcade, Conversation Piece, and three plays from Tonight at 8:30: Hands Across the Sea, Still Life, Fumed Oak) / $6.50
B462	COWARD, NOEL / Plays: Four (Blithe Spirit, Present Laughter, This Happy Breed, and three plays from Tonight at 8:30: Ways and Means, The Astonished Heart, Red Peppers) / $6.50
E159	DELANEY, SHELAGH / A Taste of Honey / $3.95
E380	DURRENMATT, FRIEDRICH / The Physicists / $2.95
E344	DURRENMATT, FRIEDRICH / The Visit / $2.95
E223	GELBER, JACK / The Connection / $3.95
E130	GENET, JEAN / The Balcony / $3.95
E208	GENET, JEAN / The Blacks: A Clown Show / $3.95
E577	GENET, JEAN / The Maids and Deathwatch: Two Plays / $3.95
B382	GENET, JEAN / Querelle / $2.95
E374	GENET, JEAN / The Screens / $4.95
E677	GRIFFITHS, TREVOR / The Comedians / $3.95
E446	HAVEL, VACLAV / The Memorandum / $5.95
E457	HERBERT, JOHN / Fortune and Men's Eyes / $4.95
B154	HOCHHUTH, ROLF / The Deputy / $3.95
E456	IONESCO, EUGENE / Exit the King / $2.95

E101   IONESCO, EUGENE / Four Plays (The Bald Soprano, The Lesson, The Chairs, Jack, or The Submission / $2.95

E613   IONESCO, EUGENE / Killing Game / $2.95

E614   IONESCO, EUGENE / Macbett / $2.95

E679   IONESCO, EUGENE / Man With Bags / $3.95

E259   IONESCO, EUGENE / Rhinoceros and Other Plays (The Leader, The Future Is in Eggs) / $2.45

E485   IONESCO, EUGENE / A Stroll in the Air and Frenzy for Two or More: Two Plays / $2.45

E496   JARRY, ALFRED / The Ubu Plays (Ubu Rex, Ubu Cuckolded, Ubu Enchained) / $4.95

B443   KAUFMAN, GEORGE S., and HART, MOSS / Once in a Lifetime, You Can't Take It With You, The Man Who Came To Dinner / $5.95

E633   LAHR, JOHN, ed. / Grove Press Modern Drama (The Toilet by Imamu Amiri Baraka [LeRoi Jones], The Caucasian Chalk Circle by Bertolt Brecht, The White House Murder Case by Jules Feiffer, The Blacks by Jean Genet, Rhinoceros by Eugene Ionesco, Tango by Slawomir Mrozek) / $5.95

E697   MAMET, DAVID / American Buffalo / $3.95

E778   MAMET, DAVID / Lakeboat / $4.95

E709   MAMET, DAVID / A Life in the Theatre / $3.95

E712   MAMET, DAVID / Sexual Perversity in Chicago and The Duck Variations: Two Plays / $3.95

E716   MAMET, DAVID / The Water Engine and Mr. Happiness / $3.95

E725   MAMET, DAVID / The Woods / $3.95

B142   McCLURE, MICHAEL / The Beard / $1.25

B107   MOON, SAMUEL, ed. / One Act: Eleven Short Plays of the Modern Theater (Miss Julie by August Strindberg, Purgatory by William Butler Yeats, The Man With the Flower in His Mouth by Luigi Pirandello, Pullman Car Hiawatha by Thornton Wilder, Hello Out There by William Saroyan, 27 Wagons Full of Cotton by Tennessee Williams, Bedtime Story by Sean O'Casey, Cecile by Jean Anouilh, This Music Crept By Me Upon the Waters by Archibald MacLeish, A Memory of Two Mondays by Arthur Miller, The Chairs by Eugene Ionesco) / $3.95

I'll Be Frank, Artist Descending a Staircase, Where Are They Now? A Separate Peace) / $3.95

E684 STOPPARD, TOM / Dirty Linen and New-Found-Land: Two Plays / $2.95

E703 STOPPARD, TOM / Every Good Boy Deserves Favor and Professional Foul: Two Plays / $3.95

E626 STOPPARD, TOM / Jumpers / $2.95

E489 STOPPARD, TOM / The Real Inspector Hound and After Magritte: Two Plays / $3.95

B319 STOPPARD, TOM / Rosencrantz and Guildenstern Are Dead / $2.25

E661 STOPPARD, TOM / Travesties / $2.95

E708 VAN ITALLIE, JEAN-CLAUDE / America Hurrah and Other Plays (The Serpent, A Fable, The Hunter and the Bird, Almost Like Being) / $5.95

E62 WALEY, ARTHUR, tr. and ed. / The No Plays of Japan / $5.95

E519 WOOD, CHARLES / Dingo / $1.95

CRITICAL STUDIES

E127 ARTAUD, ANTONIN / The Theater and Its Double / $3.95

E743 BENTLEY, ERIC / The Brecht Commentaries / $9.50

E441 COHN, RUBY, ed. / Casebook on Waiting for Godot / $4.95

E603 HARRISON, PAUL CARTER / The Drama of Nommo: Black Theater in the African Continuum / $2.45

E695 HAYMAN, RONALD / How To Read A Play / $2.95

E387 IONESCO, EUGENE / Notes and Counternotes: Writings on the Theater / $3.95

E735 KNOWLSON, JAMES and PILLING, JOHN, eds. / Frescoes of the Skull: The Later Prose and Drama of Samuel Beckett / $9.50

GROVE PRESS, INC., 196 West Houston St., New York, N.Y. 10014